"Doug Woodward, with capab[le] Krieger, is once again unafraid to polemics regarding America's 'exce[pt] status. *Uncommon Sense* is a wake-up call for conservatives and especially for evangelicals, both groups that uncritically conflate God and Country, telling the unvarnished truth about why America today has never been more threatened."

Derek P. Gilbert
Co-author, *Rise of the Cybergods* (spring 2015)
Co-host, P.I.D. (Peering into Darkness) Radio
Host, *A View from the Bunker*

"This incisive analysis opens the eyes and pierces the heart. What can we do to change the path we are following? Is it too late for America to reclaim the mantle of global leadership?"

David W. Lowe
Author of *Then His Voice Shook Earth*
www.deconstructinglucifer.com

"*Uncommon Sense* compels Americans to take an honest look at ourselves. This book provides an untold story chock full of incontrovertible facts which explains why our citizens have grown cynical about our government and why our nation lost the moral high ground in geopolitics."

Pastor Douglas Shearer
Author of *Calvin on the Ropes*
Urban Hope Prophecy Club

"For the most part, Christians have stopped studying Bible prophecy. Most evangelical pastors consider it too speculative and divisive. Seminary professors demonstrate little interest, presumably because its imagery remains incomprehensible or requires a supernatural stance that threatens their intellectualism and credibility. *Uncommon Sense* warns that shunning prophecy dismisses the apocalyptic promise of the coming Kingdom of God, waters down the power of the gospel, and invalidates the message of Jesus Christ as presented in the Bible. From another vantage point, evangelicals have implicitly adopted the Amillennial stance of Catholics, or worse, the naturalism of atheists. Very much to the peril of our society, when interest in eschatology wanes among Christians, the saltiness of Christ's followers becomes neutralized."

Gonzo Shimura
Producer, *Age of Deceit* and *Age of Deceit 2*
Director and Founder, *The Prophecy Forum*

"With added gems within crucial concepts, these essays flow together into a brand new creature: a true manifesto that is much needed in our Church and culture today."

Josh Peck
Host, *The Sharpening*
Author, *Quantum Creation*

"The book Uncommon Sense *begins by perspicuously recounting American spiritual history. Woodward shows that the mysticism of today's evangelical 'Emergent Church Movement' comprises nothing new or distinctive. It is part and parcel of our 'new world' culture. Indeed, the New Age movement began in America in the nineteenth century with Blavatsky's Theosophy; then blossomed in the twentieth century with Alice Bailey; while in the twenty-first, we witness the invasion of Buddhism undermining genuine Christian mysticism in the guise of transformative prayer techniques which discount the person of Jesus Christ. On this count alone, the cost of the book is fully justified."*

John Haller, esq.
Conference speaker, and Bible teacher/leader @
Fellowship Bible Chapel, Lewis Center, Ohio

"The tale of how America, England, and the Vatican intentionally helped foster the rise of Nazism in Germany and succored war criminals afterwards, has been taken up by a number of authors over the past four decades. The topic grows more engaging, however, as the accounts of Hitler's possible escape become more frequent and detailed. Woodward places this formerly implausible hypothesis within the context of revising America's true role before and after World War II. Our nation must face the facts: the 'uncommon sense' of growing fascism hastened by our military-industrial complex implicates our foreign policy now and undergirds the claim of Woodward and Krieger that America truly constitutes 'the final Babylon.' Uncommon Sense *provides yet more support for their alarming thesis which circulates among Bible prophecy students today."*

Rev. William W. Cotte
First Congregational Church, St. Johnsbury Center, Vermont and
Professor, Fine and Performing Arts, Lyndon State College
Lyndonville, Vermont

"Christianity is never comfortable with a false dichotomy of 'church and state.' Woodward and Krieger challenge conventional thinking typical of the evangelical community. On the one hand, they shine a light on the nature of deception in Nazi Germany and ask if the same deception is happening today in America. On the other, they excoriate the banality of the so-called Emergent Church which focuses on individual wealth, health, and personal well-being. In the spirit of Dietrich Bonhoeffer they proclaim, 'NO MORE CHEAP GRACE!' It's time for Christians who care about the gospel to challenge Babylon by embracing what Jesus really taught: the implacable Kingdom of God."

Coach Dave Daubenmire
Pass the Salt Ministries

UNCOMMON SENSE

A Prophetic Manifesto for the Church in Babylon

S. DOUGLAS WOODWARD

Foreword by Contributing Author, Douglas W. Krieger

Other Books by S. Douglas Woodward

Are We Living in the Last Days?

Decoding Doomsday

Black Sun, Blood Moon

Power Quest, Book One

Power Quest, Book Two

Lying Wonders of the Red Planet

Blood Moon

Co-authored with Douglas W. Krieger and Dene McGriff

The Final Babylon

Contributing Author:

Pandemonium's Engine

Blood on the Altar

UNCOMMON SENSE

A PROPHETIC MANIFESTO FOR THE CHURCH IN BABYLON

S. Douglas Woodward

Foreword by Contributing Author:
Douglas W. Krieger

With an Afterword by
Sharon K. Gilbert

Faith Happens
Oklahoma City

UNCOMMON SENSE

A Prophetic Manifesto for the Church in Babylon

All inquiries should be directed to Faith Happens in c/o
S. Douglas Woodward at doug@faith-happens.com.

Multiple copies may be purchased at a discount. Contact info@faith-happens.com for information and assistance.

Unless otherwise noted, all scripture taken from the King James Bible.

Woodward's web site located at www.faith-happens.com.

Contact S. Douglas Woodward via email at doug@faith-happens.com.

Facebook www.facebook.com/sdouglaswoodward

Printed in the United States of America

ISBN-13: 978-1502559203

ISBN-10: 150255920X

Cover design by Gonzo Shimura and S. Douglas Woodward

CONTENTS

Figures

To my grandchild Brody
and all future grandchildren
with which the Lord may bless me:
May you grow up in an American nation
revived and restored by returning to the King of Kings.

Acknowledgements

First, I am in gratitude to my co-author on *The Final Babylon*, and contributing author here, Douglas W. Krieger, for working with me in preparing this manuscript, and providing a superlative *Foreword* to get us off on the right foot.

Secondly, a thank you must go to Sharon K Gilbert who has grown to be a most appreciated friend who continues to inspire me with her highly intelligent contributions to the eschatology community drawn from her in depth knowledge of microbiology, genetics, and knowledge of biblical issues at the dawn of transhumanism. She was only too willing to write an *Afterword* which is much appreciated. Too often we fail to go the final mile to explain what the implications are on the topics about which we writers write. Sharon has helped overcome my deficiency in this regard.

Thirdly, thank you to Gonzo Shimura who has become a good friend over the past four months as we (along with John Haller, Gary Winkelman, and Doug Krieger) have built *The Prophecy Forum* together. Gonz provided the overall design concept for the cover. I needed a good deal of help on this one because I was stumped on how best to illustrate the essential concept of the book. I hope the reader agrees that what we eventually developed does a good job on this count. Gonzo is very talented and we, at *The Prophecy Forum*, are very blessed to have his assistance on producing our podcasts, creating our web pages, and his insisting our graphics and overall presentation convey professionalism.

Thank you to Denis Burgess for his proofing and suggestions.

Thanks to all my friends and acquaintances on providing kind words of endorsement for the message contained herein. Derek Gilbert, David Lowe, Dave Daubenmire, Douglas Shearer, William Cotte, John Haller, Josh Peck, and once more, Gonzo Shimura.

Finally, a big thank you to those who support the ministry of The Prophecy Forum and my fans who read my books! Bless you!

Foreword

By Douglas W. Krieger

"Society in every state is a blessing, but government even in its best state is but a necessary evil; in its worst state an intolerable one; for when we suffer, or are exposed to the same miseries by a government, which we might expect in a country without government, our calamity is heightened by reflecting that we furnish the means by which we suffer..."
— Thomas Paine, Common Sense

The title of this book, *Uncommon Sense*, obviously harkens back to Thomas Paine's famous and monumental book, *Common Sense*, which sparked (indeed almost carried the day for) the American Revolution. Despite being an atheist, he had much good to say. The young republic was and always will be, forever in his debt. Paine understood exactly what 'a government gone wrong' was. Tyranny is tyranny no matter its form. 'Common sense' now informs us all too well that democracies are not immune to despotism: most wealthy individuals and large-scale corporations act out of their own selfish interests while the People are oppressed. Unbridled from their pernicious influence, the nation drifts inexorably into all sorts of evils.

This book could have been entitled: *Blood on Our Hands!* Other possible titles might have been "Trafficking in the bodies and souls of men" (Rev. 18:13) and "her cup is full of putridities"—since our end-times power-hungry nation (drunken with commercial exploitation of the third-world) enters her final stages of religious perfidy, military prowess, and political confusion. S. Douglas Woodward was indeed generously influenced by his 'co-conspirators' (like this author) willingly and without reserve. I unashamedly assert, it is time for those responsible for the sinking ship (like the unheroic captain of the *Concordia* and overconfident designer of the *Titanic*) to cease offering reassuring balderdash that the ship (in our case, the country) stays afloat because all things remain the same since the beginning of time (or more recently, the genesis of this nation). No, they are not the same—the 'new normal' is destroying a once great people. Our nation has already smashed headlong into the rocks and takes on water in great gushes.

U.S. President Barak Obama (whose popularity most political pundits acknowledge *is* sinking fast), once again asserts our vaunted intelligence community has failed to warn our country of the pervasive dangers of ISIS—a "JV (Junior Varsity) of Jihadists" according to the initial analysis communicated so confidently by Obama. Despite their supposed sophomoric status, ISIS continues on (unraveling the Iraqi state that cost U.S. taxpayers one trillion dollars), unbelievably racing across the desert in left-behind US military equipment, and crucifying hundreds (if not thousands) of Christians *there* (while Jihadists whom they've inspired, now behead Americans *here*!) Furthermore, adding insult to injury, the Obama administration (as this book is published) refuses to acknowledge the blatant fact that their belated response, a cautious and constrained "air war" against ISIS, is still—nevertheless—a WAR!

Isaiah 24 speaks of the final judgment of the nations; but one in particular that is especially confounded—the once great city: *"Therefore the curse has devoured the earth, and those who dwell in it are held guilty . . . therefore the inhabitants of the earth are burned, and few men are left . . . The City of Confusion is broken down . . . in the City Desolation is left, and the gate is stricken with destruction"* (Isaiah 24:6, 10, 12).

Listen up, S. Douglas Woodward (with a little help from this friend), is about to methodically dismantle whatever you once thought about 'God's grace (being) shed (any longer) on thee from sea to shining sea'—instead, the rise of Antichrist now wafts from shore to shore. We witness the proliferation of 'wars and rumors of wars,' plagues of Biblical proportion, signs in the heavens and on the earth... for within this glittering city once set on a hill are all manner of lasciviousness, greed, murder... a veritable cornucopia of forbidden fruit freely consumed by those that dwell upon this portion of earthly clod. For the party goers are oblivious to the teeming and impoverished masses clamoring outside her walls. And worse, her leadership and compliant 'sheeple' are blinded and dumbfounded to the weird handwriting emblazoned upon the walls of their decadent ball, as well as to the relevance of the Almighty's thunderous outburst through His beloved prophet Daniel:

> *"God has numbered your kingdom, and finished it; you have been weighed in the balances, and found wanting...your kingdom has been divided"* (Dan. 5:26-28).

Neither shall you be capable of buying off those who illuminate your decrepit condition. Those of us who would be 'salt and light' in this diseased and darkened despair (once glistening with the radiance of order, honor and integrity), are now being called upon to 'stand and deliver' one last call for humankind to change its ways: "Repent and accept divine deliverance through Christ, the Messiah, and coming King of kings and Lord of lords, before it is too late." Mock, if you must (and many shall), but know this full well: only divine intervention can provide escape from the wrath to come.

"Multitudes, multitudes in the Valley of Decision, for the Day of the Lord, is near, in the Valley of Decision" (Joel 3:14). By the time you finish this book, you'll be forced to make a decision . . . may it count for eternity! The Judge of all the earth cometh—and He's not a happy camper. In other words perhaps more apropos, the party's over and the festooned hall lies darkened. Indeed, the pretty balloons in red, white, and blue are destined to go 'pop' any moment now.

Douglas W. Krieger

Director, The Prophecy Forum and Editor, Co-editor TribNet.org
Author, *Signs in the Heaven and On the Earth*

Sacramento, October 2014

Introduction

I have never thought of myself being particularly political. I have even gone so far to regard myself as *apolitical*. True, like most other Oklahomans I grew up in a very Republican family. So I have always veered to the right of center. Certainly I have never registered as a Democrat (heaven forbid!) When I reregister to vote in Oklahoma (having been absent from the state for 27 years), I likely will register as an Independent—although if I thought being a Libertarian would do anybody any good, I might be tempted to go that direction.

As a Christian writer, I had always intended to keep my writing focused on biblical topics and avoid getting too deeply embroiled in political controversy. This was partly because I believed that I should talk about that which I know the most and avoid subjects about which I know very little. Of course, when one turns 60 (which I did this summer), most everyone thinks he or she has automatically become an expert about politics. I am no different. The school of hard knocks does teach some valuable lessons. *Political reality* stands out as one of those subjects. Consequently, I am not as shy regarding my political point of view as I was, say, ten years ago. As far as what comprises good government, I find myself writing more and more about the *implications* of what I believe (and no doubt what most who read my books would agree makes sense too). Furthermore, I affirm that separating one's religion and politics remains nigh unto impossible if such a one's perspective on spiritual truth really amounts to much.

Such self-analysis became vividly apparent to me during the past year as I wrote a number of new books and updated some earlier ones. It dawned on me that for the benefit of those who have not read my earlier books or may not have yet had time to pick up any of my recent titles, that I should compile the most essential chapters (I call them essays here) forming something of a *manifesto*, as Webster defines it—*a statement of policy and principles for public consumption.* A manifesto is invariably *political*.

Therefore, before you rests a compendium drawn from five of my most topical books and a recently penned article. In essence, it comprises what I (1) assert biblically-oriented believers should understand about America (and likely do not know) which would overturn widespread falsehoods about our country, as well as (2) set forth the agenda that the true Church of Jesus Christ should pursue in the months and years just ahead—*if, that is,* we would have a meaningful impact on society before the Lord Jesus returns to establish His Kingdom.

My co-authors Douglas W. Krieger (a great researcher and deep thinker), along with Dene McGriff (an economic expert with decades of real-world experience) teamed with yours truly to write *The Final Babylon: America and the Coming of Antichrist* (2013). That book continues to sell well—and its biggest selling days *may still lie ahead.* In *The Final Babylon,* we argue that the United States of America constitutes the last and most powerful version of numerous 'Babylons' discussed and prophesied in the Scripture. Co-opting an oft-heard phrase, we argue that the USA does stand out as truly *the indispensable nation*—but in its proper context, *indispensable* as far as the *New World Order* is concerned. While admittedly controversial, supporters of the book have far outnumbered detractors, almost 20-to-1 based on public comments we have received. Two of those most hard-hitting chapters (written jointly by Krieger and me) have been updated and included here. One of them was also recently published in Tom Horn's *Blood on the Altar: The Coming War between Christian vs. Christian* (2014). That book is destined to stir the kettle too. At this moment (late summer 2014), it is becoming a break-out bestseller.

One of the essays here discusses the place of the United States as the catalyzing nation-state engaged for almost one hundred years as protagonist for global government. This mission is sometimes equated with *Democratic Globalism* (a phrase taken from a speech by Charles Krauthammer, syndicated columnist), and other times as *Corporatism*. Its reality, however, constitutes a 'kinder, gentler form of fascism' (to borrow and abuse a line from the Grand Poobah of the New World Order himself, President George H.W. Bush, aka 'Poppy,' aka '41'). The second joint-essay also connects the status of America's 'church and state' with the condition existing in Germany during the run-up to World War II. We pose the question, "When (not if) the Antichrist appears in America, will we (the Church of Jesus Christ) recognize him?" Thanks to the in depth research of friend and co-author Douglas Krieger presented in this essay, we recognize how the Fuehrer co-opted the Catholics and Protestants in Germany by distinguishing (falsely) the spheres of politics from religion. By emphasizing that preachers and priests should pastor their flocks and avoid commenting on governmental policies or politics, Hitler effectively silenced the Church and eventually reworked the nature of Christianity and Christ. Jesus became a blond haired, blue-eyed Aryan whose teaching was transformed into anti-Semitic diatribe. Krieger and I ponder whether today's most famous Megachurches and pop-preachers of prosperity will unwittingly eventuate the same outcome.

Before the reader encounters those two chapters, three other essays are presented that provide a brief but crucial history of (1) America's fascination with the paranormal (culled from *Power Quest Book One: America's Obsession with the Paranormal*) and (2) the history of how German fascism (read: Nazism) was imported into the Americas owing to the U.S. government, the Vatican, and Wall Street bankers (drawn from *Power Quest Book Two: The Ascendancy of Antichrist in America*).

The two *Power Quest* books contain a vast amount of research, together consisting of over 200,000 words (800 pages) and therefore remain daunting for the average booklover. On behalf of the common reader, I strive here to make accessible some of the most important (and I hope intriguing) material from the two *Power Quest* books. This material provided a foundation for what followed.

I titled this work *Uncommon Sense* partly because the material covered in these first three essays demands the attention of all *serious* Christians in America (are real Christians anything less?) Written before *The Final Babylon*, I sought to build a mammoth if not stalwart case for why America, despite its many laudable traits and inspiring beginning, had also 'been up to no good.' I argued that since the beginning of the twentieth century, the USA often wore the black hat. As the century progressed, the decline of America's ethics and republican (i.e., Jeffersonian) sentiment faded, until it became 'the heavy'—dominating the globe through economic and military bullying. Drawing out this material once again in this volume, I seek to provide the reader with the necessary vantage point to judge for themselves whether America really does comprise 'The Final Babylon' of these last days. The ultimate question remains: When Jesus Christ returns to set up His Kingdom, will the world system he overturns be the New World Order? Will this final Babylon be centered in the megalopolis that stretches from Boston to Washington, with New York City its economic and cultural heart? Will the United States be primarily accountable to the God of the Bible for its destructive effects upon the souls of men?

The last two essays are adapted from my two most recent books, *Lying Wonders of the Red Planet: Exposing the Lie of Ancient Aliens (2014)* and *Blood Moon: Biblical Signs of the Coming Apocalypse (2014)*. Both essays shift the focus *from* what Bible believing Christians should realize about America past's and present (the first five essays) *to* what they should recognize as the agenda for 'the church in Babylon' during these last days before Christ comes back.

My warning in *Lying Wonders*: the Church stands neither willing nor able to deal with the Evil One's *most sophisticated threat yet devised*. My point is, given the impact our love affair with the planet Mars has had on our culture for over 150 years, 'we should have seen it coming.' In the absence of a belief *in* a transcendent, supernatural

God who made the earth, sun, and stars (inasmuch as the dominant scientific view of our society for over a century has been *atheism*), many have chosen instead to fill this gap with a *natural god from the stars* to whom they attribute our genesis. In other words, *Lying Wonders* addresses the infatuation our culture has with extraterrestrial origins. It challenges the growing belief that God consists of nothing more than what our once primitive minds devised as an explanation for extraterrestrial super-intelligences that purportedly visited our planet and nurtured our species. My research addresses the intense captivation humankind bestowed upon Mars especially since about 1875—which was a prelude to the fascination society holds for all things *outer space* today. My discussion of this arcane (and for some readers no doubt *outlandish*) subject proposes that when the Antichrist appears, he may assert that ET was in fact our species' forebear and that he, the Antichrist, has a personal connection with 'them'—not just spiritual but more inherently *genetic*. In effect, the 'man of lawlessness' will offer a value proposition that comprises the final great deception of 2 Thessalonians 2:8, 9. Despite the outrageous nature of this assertion, many authors who write on prophetic topics today completely agree. If this prediction does come true, I contend the Church better had prepared its response *beforehand*. To do otherwise, amounts to our falling asleep at the wheel. It was on this very matter that Jesus expressly warned His disciples, *"If it were possible even the elect of God would be deceived. Note that I have told you ahead of time. So be on your guard."* (Mark 13:22, Matthew 24:24, my paraphrase)

In the even more recent book *Blood Moon,* I demonstrate that the excitement biblical students in eschatology hold for the contemporary 'tetrads'—the four 'blood moons' occurring on two consecutive Jewish High Holy Days (that is, Passover and Sukkot during 2014 and 2015) constitutes a *practicable* sign of the imminent apocalypse. While any authentic case for affirming these naturally occurring events would demand they be *providential* signs presaging the end of the days, at the very least, they remind us of the apocalyptic nature of the gospel. The Kingdom of God was Jesus' dominant message at the outset of His ministry. His was not just a message about personal piety and individual spirituality. Nor did it consist of mere proverbs promising personal happiness. It had radical social implications and dramatic cultural consequences too. This was the real Jesus. He did not mince words. Ironically, liberal scholars affirm this to be so while evangelicals dismiss it. *Apocalypticism is not 'seeker friendly.'*

This recognition requires the immediate attention of the Church, a Church which once held that the Second Coming of Christ was *fundamental* to the meaning of the Christian religion. Since the beginning of the twenty-first century, in the Evangelical Church the apocalyptic aspect of the gospel has often been downplayed if not out-and-out ridiculed. In stark contrast, I argue that the Kingdom of God must be returned to its rightful place as the *essential* message of Jesus Christ. The Kingdoms of this world are soon to be overturned. A great reversal of fortune now stands outside the door ready to knock the door down. Our most solemn agenda in these last days consists in proclaiming this *apocalypse*—this revelation—of a sudden cataclysmic transformation of human civilization inaugurated by the King of Kings. But please understand—I am not preaching the social gospel. 'Getting right with God' individually is the highest priority.

And yet, this transformation begins with the personal repentance of the individual as well as 'the collective'—it begins with a recognition that our problems stem from the evil that lurks within each of us and inevitably within the structure of those institutions we erect. Until Jesus Christ comes to live in our hearts and to reign in our midst—to root out that evil individually and corporately—there will be no enduring change within ourselves or our society. To be clear: The transformation of the individual involves a *supernatural* change.

Consequently, and in conclusion, the gospel of Jesus Christ demands dramatic conversion both in what transpires in our society and within our distinctive persons. To quote John the Baptist, we must demonstrate the fruit of repentance (Matthew 3:8). If we have been radically transformed by the Spirit of the Living Christ, if we have been truly born again, if we now have Christ in us "the hope of glory"—it will be then revealed to us what evidence we must provide of that change and what works we must then do. To be clear, this knowledge comes not of ourselves. It comes from on high. It is revealed. It is not common. *Therefore, it is* **uncommon sense** *that constitutes what we must profess if we would truly experience salvation and have a saving effect upon others.*

The gospel tells us that the coming of Jesus Christ is the blessed hope of the Church. We should be *"looking for the coming of our great God and Savior, Jesus Christ"* (Titus 2:13). Furthermore, the Apostle John reminds us why having a commitment to the 'apocalyptic' remains crucial to authentic Christianity—in short, it is a means to sanctification—*to become like Jesus.* John says, *"And every man that hath this hope in him purifieth himself, even as he is pure."* (1 John 3:3)

The world that exists today—which seemingly grows darker day by day, with fewer and fewer in its population who truly seek to become like Jesus—is a world ripe for conquering by Antichrist. That which restrains him, once taken out of the way, opens the door for his coming. Is this what the Apostle Paul meant, at least in part, when he said: *"For the mystery of lawlessness is already at work; only he who now restrains will do so until he is taken out of the way"*? (2 Thessalonians 2:7) Yes, this verse comprises a strong argument for a rapture before the appearance of Antichrist. However, have we given much thought to the possibility that as the percentage of the world's truly Christian population decreases, the impact of the gospel diminishes and the Spirit of Antichrist grows stronger? How long then will it be before he appears? His *apocalyptō* lurks.

S. Douglas Woodward

Oklahoma City

October, 2014

UNCOMMON SENSE

A Brief History of Spiritualism in America

By S. Douglas Woodward

"There are more things in heaven and earth, Horatio,
than are dreamt of in your philosophy."

William Shakespeare, _Hamlet—Act 1, scene 5_

"The world is infested, just now, by a new sect of philosophers, who have not yet
suspected themselves of forming a sect, and who, consequently, have adopted
no name. They are the Believers in Everything Old."

Edgar Allan Poe, from "Fifty Suggestions"

"It is no indulgence in hyperbole to suggest that the modern origins of America
are spiritual (or, at least, religious) in nature, and that America has spent the
last five hundred years trying—usually unsuccessfully—to ignore that fact."

Peter Levenda, _Sinister Forces_

This essay is drawn from _Power Quest, Book One: America's Obsession with the Paranormal_

IN THIS ESSAY, WE EXPLORE THE HISTORY OF THE PARANORMAL IN AMERICA, DEMONSTRATING THAT THE CURRENT INTEREST IN MYSTICISM WITHIN EVANGELICALISM DOES NOT CONSTITUTE A NEW INSIGHT, BUT EMPLOYS VERY OLD FICTION AND WILL LEAD TO MANY FATAL ERRORS.

The Witch Doctor Next Door

In today's version of what Aldous Huxley called the *perennial philosophy* (aka, pantheism), the core ideology within the self-identified New Age Movement, [1] there resounds loud accolades for shamanism. [2] Daniel Pinchbeck, author of two relevant books on the subject, *Breaking Open the Head*, and *2012:*

The Return of Quetzalcoatl, promotes the importance of shamanism as rediscovered at the close of the twentieth century. He regards shamanism as one means (if not the primary means) to transform humanity's awareness in the now passé movement we know as "2012." "The exploration and unbiased study of these mind-expanding molecules—an interrupted legacy of scientific and psychological research begun in the 1950s and shut down with hysterical force during the late 1960s—is the one way to unify these opposite approaches [brain-based *materialism* versus spirit-oriented *shamanism*] to the nature of reality. Perhaps it is the only way." [3] Pinchbeck, also a follower of the early twentieth century German white magician Rudolf Steiner, calls for the use of hallucinogenic drugs, such as mescaline or the more exotic *ayuhusca*, a ritual drink of South American occult practitioners, to help "break open the head." (Walter Stein's testimony—recorded by Trevor Ravenscroft in *The Spear of Destiny*—was that Hitler began his personal "power quest" in like manner using mescaline to contact the spirit world).

Another popular author of alternative history, Graham Hancock, echoes the same sentiment. In his 2007 book *Supernatural,* Hancock offers this definition of *shamanism:* "Shamanism is not confined to specific socio-economic settings or stages of development. It is fundamentally the ability that all of us share, some with and some without the help of hallucinogens, to enter altered states of consciousness and to travel out of body in non-physical realms—there to *encounter supernatural entities and gain useful knowledge and healing powers from them.*" [Emphasis added] [4] The important element to catch in Hancock's statement is how we should encounter mentoring entities, which is more ominous than experiencing only a feeling of euphoria. Hancock praises the 'persons' we experience in these hallucinogenic states, since in his assessment, having their own distinct intelligence *they exist to teach us about ourselves and the cosmos.* Thus, Hancock blithely assumes these intelligences are beneficent.

Whether we trust these phenomena or deny their existence drives our core interpretation of the universe. Our perspective on the nature of reality is known as *cosmology*. [5] It is "the branch of astronomy dealing with the general structure and evolution of the universe." [6] If psychic phenomena do in fact exist, our understanding of humankind and the universe can no longer be a staid *naturalism*—we must adopt a traditional supernatural view or we migrate toward the "new reality." (As discussed in *Power Quest, Book Two*, there are many in the military who accept this "fantastic reality" as pure fact, upon which some military intelligence operations can and apparently have been based, namely *remote viewing*).

Shamanism, the most ancient of religions, connects us to cultures of indigenous tribes worldwide. Shamanism relies upon highly specialized plant compounds containing hallucinogenic drugs. [7] *Shaman* is the politically correct name for *witch doctor* or *medicine man*, as the Shaman understands the various uses of plants and their ability to heal both physical and psychological conditions. But most notably, Shamans are the priests of animism and facilitate contact with the spiritual realm. In fact, a whole new tourist industry exists, (popular for the past two decades), in South America and Mexico focused on seekers of spiritual experiences using organic drugs with Shamanic oversight. Psychic experiences *south of the border* has become a chic method for the religiously disenfranchised to find their way back to some manner of spiritual encounter. While extreme, it is hardly without precedent.

Indeed, the trek is hardly a new one. Timothy Leary, the Harvard professor disillusioned with western society, became the most famous drug detective to go south in order to experience the effects of magical mushrooms. And he wasn't the first investigator. Leary was preceded by R. Gordon Wasson, a famous mycologist (*mycology* being the study of fungi). Interestingly, Wasson had been invited to work for the CIA in the early 1950s as part of the infamous and ill-fated MKULTRA project (discussed in depth in *Power Quest, Book Two*). Wasson refused the invitation; nevertheless without his knowing, he was funded by the Geshcikter Foundation for Medical Research (a CIA cover), completing his Mexican expedition in 1956. According to Pinchbeck, Wasson retains to this day the title of the father of magical mushrooms. It was indeed Wasson's 1957 article in *Life Magazine* that caught the attention of Leary and compelled him to take his very own magical mystery tour in 1960. [8] Eventually, Leary picked a different drug of choice, LSD, and become an adamant provocateur and strident promoter of hallucinogenic substances, representing them as the needed savior of Western culture. As he famously said, "Turn on, tune in, and drop out." [9] With such glowing words of wisdom, no wonder Nixon's Silent Majority of the 1960s—70s disinherited academia.

The late Terence K. McKenna, perhaps the most revered leader of the 2012 movement (as this author refers to it—a well-founded label for the ill-fated and most recent incarnation of the '*New Age*'), would have easily agreed with this assessment. Indeed, he believed that plant-based hallucinogens were the source of humanity's higher consciousness and, ultimately, the impetus for one of its most distinctive features; namely, *language*. Being two of the often-cited traits of the image of God (the *imago dei*) in humankind, the creative power attributed to mushrooms and to these chlorophyll-infused life forms transform humanity to express the divine. What remains ironic, of course, is how far outside standard reality the hallucinogens push those subjects who ingest them. Arguing that *drugs open the door to humanity's distinctiveness*—even divinity—in the author's way of thinking, supposes a leap in illogic that many spiritually-minded and non-discerning in America (even within evangelical churches) now embrace.

The surprising development of medicine men to complement other forms of holistic treatment hardly constitutes the only stunning development regarding this not-so-new way to look at the world. As demonstrated, when we turn to academics, astronomers, mathematicians, and cosmologists in today's academia, we discover how often they no longer hold reality (nature that is) to be an interaction of mere matter and energy, made known to us through the medium of space-time. As we discussed in *Power Quest, Book One*, nature is far more mysterious than the enlightened mind is willing to accept. This modern scientific approach to the 'new reality' decrees much more than physics enlivened with a dose of spiritual thinking. The new cosmology embraces the burgeoning occult views discussed above and other examples enthusiastically celebrated in America's pop culture.

As it turns out, the latest trend toward shamanism boasts perhaps the most concentrated form of such esoteric and mystical religion. It offers the greatest advocacy for individuals seeking personal power to learn techniques enabling encounter and engagement with supernatural entities—just as Hancock advises. For Hancock and so many others suffused with New Age sentiments, it is through these choice encounters we freely subordinate ourselves to the "teachers of mankind" who (supposedly) have taught *spiritual truth* to us for thousands of years as well as proffering humankind's *raison d'être*. [10] Hancock's startling advice boggles the minds of those aware of the darkened and less recommended roads who rightly remain suspicious of personal encounters with mysterious strangers there.

For those outside the circle of the initiated, it remains difficult to grasp the powerful encounter these experimenters have enjoyed. As Peter Levenda states in his study of *the doors of perception*, "those who have not taken LSD (or other hallucinogens... such as mescaline and psilocybin) cannot appreciate the effects these substances have on one's perception of reality. [Yet] those who have taken the drugs are often considered to be in no position to be objective about them!" [11] In other words, the irony stands insurmountable: without trying it, you can't know if you like it. But if you try it and like it—then you can't be objective. Therefore, once favorably disposed (based on personal experience), you ought not to try to convince others why they should follow suit. One wonders if such a moral imperative to keep quiet comes with the encounter, since most experimenters can't wait to share what they've learned.

However, it is the history of *the personal power quest* in America we wish to address in this essay. This power quest has a distinctly American character. This amazing history illustrates that American fascination with *spiritualism* (or *spiritism* as it is sometimes called) dominates our religious past far more than many presume. It continues today in surprising places.

Indeed, rather than a follower, America proved to be a leader and trend-setter in *pop religion* for almost 300 years, especially as our global influence increased. The identity of *Mystery Babylon* has been presumed by Protestants to be Roman Catholicism. Others argue it is English Freemasonry. In the last 200 years, however, America has absconded with this ill-reputed moniker. It now remains tucked away safely in America's possession.

Today, spiritualism continues to be a universal ideology surging within intellectual and pseudo-intellectual circles. What we will learn in our brief rundown of spiritualism in America over the past two centuries: although spiritualism commenced in Europe during the Renaissance it was nurtured in America until returning to Europe in the form of Theosophy late in the nineteenth century. The stunning worldwide sway of America's spiritualist movement becomes all the more astounding when one uncovers its humble origins in rural New York from the 1820s through 1870s. [12]

Mormon Magic

Peter Levenda's study on occult aspects of American politics includes a pithy analysis of the founding of Mormonism—that distinctive American take on Christianity—which encapsulates many aspects of the interplay between religion, politics, and the supernatural in America. Levenda writes,

> Joseph Smith was actively involved in the use of ritual magic—ceremonial magic—for the purpose of finding buried treasure. Like a Yankee Doctor Faustus, Joseph Smith conjured spirits to come to his aid. With amulets and talismans, pentacles and swords, sigils and

strange alphabets, he stepped from the misty milieu of Continental European magic and into the creation of the quintessential American-born religion, a religion which ties together some loose ends of American archaeology, Christian cabala, Freemasonry, and old-fashioned Bible stories to weave a crazy quilt of millennial paranoia, pseudo-Egyptian magic, and Masonic ritual. In fact, Joseph Smith could be considered one of the godfathers of the American occult scene, the progenitor of such groups as the Church of Satan, the OTO 'Caliphate,' even the witchcraft revival of the 1970s. [13]

While Joseph Smith initially followed in his father's footsteps using a divining rod and seer stone to find buried treasure, his interests eventually turned to more esoteric matters. He became fascinated with magic stones and gazed endlessly into them. Soon he was seeing visions. Might the finding of the famous golden plates in 1823 (with the aid of the angel *Moroni*) have been the byproduct of his honed visionary skill? It is true that several years would go by before he would use seer stones to translate the tablets into the *Book of Mormon*. But Smith's fondness for the mystical continued throughout. Soon it became obvious that the *realm of the spirit* had bigger things in store for Mr. Smith than simply uncovering colored stones whose use constituted a divine pair of dice. His pietistic persistence led to encounters with personal forces eagerly guiding him to new and many times puzzling enchantments.

Most Mormons have no idea just how *magical* Smith was. Not only did he grow up in a family of occult practitioners (a channeling mother, a wizard father, as well as an aunt who married an alchemist), he continued practicing ritual magic even after he had founded Mormonism and had written the *Book of Mormon*. Smith led a team of followers into Salem, Massachusetts, a town well-acquainted with magic and witchcraft, seeking hoped-for treasure supposedly hidden in a house there. This incident was in 1836, six years after completing his epic religious revelation on the visitation of Christ to America and the elimination of a white race descended from the lost tribes of Israel. Despite Smith's best efforts in Salem, no treasure was found. After this failure, his focus would be centered mostly on church building until he was murdered in 1844. Perhaps he found the pay better from collecting consistent offerings drawn from his congregations rather than the occasionally *divined* unearthed treasure.

D. Michael Quinn in his seminal study *Early Mormonism and the Magic World View* provided this important insight:

> Joseph Smith's family owned magical charms, divining rods, amulets, a ceremonial dagger inscribed with astrological symbols of Scorpio and seals of Mars, and parchments marked with occult signs and cryptograms popular in eighteenth- and nineteenth-century English and American folklore. In her 1845 Oral memoir, the family matriarch, Lucy Mack Smith, recalled the Smith's interest in "the faculty of *Abrac*"—a term that might have been lost on some. In fact, *Abrac*, or *Abraxas*, is a Gnostic Term for God that also served as a magical incantation. It forms the root of a magic word known to every child: *abracadabra*.

Quinn also indicates that in the period after the War of 1812, the number of occult books in America multiplied. A listing of various occult books in print or available second-hand from that era was over 100 pages! [14] The availability of this material to Smith was no doubt useful as he envisioned his religion and brought it to life.

Smith's spiritualist point of view can best be summarized as an amalgamation of select borrowings from Christian doctrine, inspiration attributable to American ingenuity, and the fanciful practice of magical ceremonies. Additionally, when in 1842 Smith was initiated into Freemasonry he obtained substantial new material for devising his religious views. At the end of the day, Smith was nothing if not a solid American pragmatist, being eminently real-world about religious matters. Even the polygamist path was a practical revelation. After all, keeping as many wives pregnant as possible couldn't help but grow the movement until the latter days were come.

10

We must ask, "Weren't all these forms of supernaturalism related by the simple fact they were all spiritual pursuits?" And the follow-up question: "Why would there need be any distinction drawn between one form of spiritual practice from another?" In America, the guiding principle seems to be, "*If it works, it must be right.*" As Levenda notes, the Smiths "seemed to be firm believers and... were religious people as well, for whom their occult practices were perceived as complementary—rather than in opposition—to their Christian faith." [15] Levenda's analysis continues with these words:

> Magic was believed to be an extension of religion, and not in opposition to it. Thus, we have many clergymen, scientists, and political leaders involved in those days in practices that can only seem unsavory today. To be sure, many strict fundamentalists opposed to the practice of magic, fearing that it would lead to the excesses of witchcraft and demon-worship. But to the farmer, the villager, the blacksmith, these practices were based on a system of knowledge that was gleaned from the stars and the phases of the moon, things of nature, things that regulated their lives anyway and told them when to plant and when to harvest. [16]

In short, American religion was not particularly discriminating when it came to doctrinal distinctions. Just as certain Renaissance theologians [17] came to believe that Hermeticism and Christian doctrine should be blended into a composite ideology that would make it more amenable to parties outside the circle of Christian faith, American religion was eager to unite rather than divide spiritual views which shared a regard for supernatural or mystical realities. [18] Such a pluralist approach to religion can't help but be politically correct—even if it winds up being dribble. *(NOTE: This axiom constitutes the core driver of mysticism in the evangelical church today. Doctrine divides—the indescribable abides).*

This tendency to *synthesize*, rather than *distinguish* religious views which oppose one another, contributes to the next spiritualist trend, appearing as it does as another intriguing blip on our radar.

American Occultism and Social Good

Although a Christian who proudly traffics in evangelical circles, the author is cautious when it comes to labeling opposing views with extreme remarks. [19] For instance, to make everyone who participates in personal occultism, mysticism, or spiritualism out to be a Satanist would be philosophically naïve and historically inaccurate. Human sociology and psychology are much more complex than this label connotes and any sincere investigation disavows overly simplistic analysis. Plus, name calling fails to advance the discussion nor factually present the historical record for those characters whose story we seek to accurately portray. This is not to say that the ultimate origins of occultist inclinations cannot be assigned to evil personages, particularly when horrific self-serving aspects of spiritualism are center stage and moral judgments are mandated from concerned and sympathetic people. The Nazis illustrated the worst in spiritualism by amassing these preternatural resources for evil purposes. Examples provided by those close to the action clearly illustrate just how wicked spiritualism without a moral compass becomes. [20] In stark contrast, American spiritualism remains more subtle. *Historically, it possesses a strong moral and socially informed compass.* Doctrinally, this makes it all the more dangerous. *Behold Lucifer—the illuminated angel of darkness!*

Throughout his astute analysis of the occult in America, Mitch Horowitz makes this point plain:

> In the public mind, the occultist craved immortality, deific power, and limitless knowledge. It was an image that popular occultists often fed. The nineteenth-century French magician Eliphas Levi [1810-1875] fancied the occult arts "a science which confers on man *powers apparently superhuman.*" [Emphasis added] England's 'Great Beast' Aleister Crowley extolled self-gratification in his best-known maxim: "Do what thou wilt shall be the whole of the law."
>
> The Standard-bearers of the American occult took a different path. They sought to remake mystical ideas *as tools of public good and self-*

help. The most influential trance medium of the nineteenth century, Andrew Jackson Davis—called the 'Poughkeepsie Seer' after his Hudson Valley, New York, home—enthralled thousands with visions of heaven as a place that included all the world's people: black, white, Indian, and followers of every religion. In early America, the occult and liberalism were closely joined, especially in the movement of Spiritualism—or contacting the dead—whose newspapers and practitioners were ardently abolitionist and suffragist. For women, Spiritualist practices, from séances to spirit channeling, became vehicles for the earliest forms of religious and political leadership. [21] [Emphasis added]

Horowitz documents a particularly colorful example of how women rode the spiritualist religion to public prominence in his account of the 1872 presidential campaign of trance-medium Victoria Woodhull, from the Equal Rights Party, "a consortium of Suffragists and abolitionists:"

Woodhull had gained national prominence the previous year in a historic voting-rights speech before the congressional Judiciary Committee. She was the first woman to appear before a joint committee of Congress. She later told supporters that the Woodhull Memorial, as her testimony was known, had been dictated to her in a dream by a ghostly, tunic-wearing Greek elder—a spiritual guardian who had guided all of her public utterances ever since she was a little girl. Woodhull's presidential campaign was quixotic and short-lived, quickly eclipsed by her twin passions for publicity-mongering and political chicanery. The medium-activist selected Frederick Douglass as her running mate—but without asking him. "I never heard of this," the abolitionist hero later said. [22]

It is also plain that most American practitioners of mysticism, occultism, channeling, et al, *saw their spiritualism as a Christian vocation. They recognized no conflict.* "In the Church's zeal to erase the old practices—practices that had endured throughout the late ancient world (even Rome's first Christian emperor, Constantine, personally combined Christianity with sun worship)—bishops branded pantheists and nature worshippers, astrologers and cosmologists, cultists and soothsayers in ways that such believers had never conceived of themselves: as practitioners of Satanism and black magic." [23] Horowitz's perspective, of course, is distinctly pluralist. [24] He offers no philosophical critique about occultism amidst his otherwise lucid analysis of its history in the USA.

In summing up the matter, we read, "So heavily did the lines between progressive politics and Spiritualism intersect in the nineteenth century that it was rare to find a leader in one field who had not at least a passing involvement in the other." [25] It is seldom true that anyone sufficiently committed to their spiritual beliefs feels political action is improper or disingenuous. Indeed the opposite stands true: *in America, spirituality should result in political action; otherwise the veracity of spiritual or religious commitment will be questioned.* The broad wall erected by the mainline media betwixt politics and religion in this country during the past few decades, (presumed mandatory due to the separation of church and state), contrasts starkly to the spiritual and political temperament of our country since its inception. Church and State may be distinct. But religious conviction without social consequence doesn't fly here.

Often we hear the question, "What would Jesus do?" Those who read the gospels carefully deny that He would 'sit on the sidelines.' *Jesus was an activist as well as a pietist.* Faith and works—working together—are the sure signs of salvation. Of that we testify.

At the conversion of the tax collector (a 'publican,' Zacchaeus from Jericho—see Luke 19:1-10—the most hated public official in town), once he pledged to repay what he had stolen from the citizens of his region, *then* Jesus proclaimed "Truly has salvation come to this house." Likewise, social good, even if performed by those whose doctrine is woefully errant, remains worthy of praise. With that being said, we must be cautious regarding the reverse: worthy actions—no matter how meritorious—do not correct mistaken theology. Nor do they excuse misleading the children of God. In other words, *good works no matter how well intended or effective, should never excuse bad theology.* One magnanimous deed does not make a wrong-headed notion right.

America's Most Influential Medium

Few in American religious circles today have heard of *Andrew Jackson Davis* (1826-1910), the namesake of the seventh American President. Born to an upstate New York family, Jackson's impact upon history constitutes a genuine enigma. The fact that he was born in rural New York and returned to New York City in later years surfaces a key aspect of the origin of America's spiritualist movement. As celebrated in Washington Irving's tale of the headless horseman in "The Legend of Sleepy Hollow" (an upper state New York village), *rural New York comprises the spiritual focal point in America for most cults that combine Christianity and spiritualism.* [26] One might say the coincidence of so many cults arising from this area comprises something of 'the inexplicable' in and of itself.

Andrew Jackson Davis was influenced by local tales of witchcraft, ghosts, and spiritism that pervaded the region. His mother spoke of dreams and visions. Eventually the family moved to Poughkeepsie (hence, his nickname—the 'Poughkeepsie Seer'). It was however, the influence of the esoteric German—Franz Anton Mesmer—

Figure 1 - Andrew Jackson Davis 1847

that would set Davis on his mystical course.

Mesmer resembled the classic alchemist; he spoke of the *aether* (the universal medium purportedly existent throughout all space-time) with a slightly different twist. To him, the aether involved 'animal magnetism' a dynamic life force animating all of nature. Mesmer even partially *personified* the aether. He enthralled many in the European monarchy (who always possessed time to dabble in the occult) with his ability to put a person into a trance state—literally *mesmerizing* them. Marquis de Lafayette, George Washington's French ally, was passionate about Mesmer.

Horowitz quotes Lafayette's letter to Washington penned in Paris on May 14, 1784: "A German doctor called Mesmer having made the greatest discovery upon *Magnetism Animal*, he has instructed scholars, among whom your humble servant is called one of the most enthusiastic—I know as much as any conjuror ever did... and before I go, I will get leave to let you into the secret of Mesmer, which you may depend upon, is a grand philosophical discovery." [27] In fact Lafayette carried a letter from Mesmer himself to personally place in Washington's hands. In typical diplomatic fashion, Washington politely replied to Mesmer, after receiving a thorough explanation from Lafayette, "[If] the powers of magnetism... should prove as extensively beneficial as it is said it will, [it] must be fortunate indeed for mankind, and redound very highly to the honor of that genius to whom it owes its birth." [28]

In 1843, Horowitz relates how a traveling Mesmerist found An-

Figure 2 - Franz Anton Mesmer

drew Jackson Davis an eager volunteer, easily placed into a trance state (obviously a technique like, if not identical, to hypnosis). Davis described this state with words oozing euphoria and sentimentality (e.g., 'a lightness of being'). After an especially mystical experience involving the appearance of the dead Swedish mystic, Emanuel Swedenborg (1688-1772, his appearance in Davis' vision being *ghostly* of course), Davis felt compelled to deliver "lectures on religious or metaphysical topics while in a trance, or *magnetized*, state. He claimed his ideas came from higher regions which he could visit in his psychical flights [no doubt similar to the *out of body* and *remote viewing* I discuss at length in *Power Quest, Book Two*]. In fact, Davis determined he would dictate an entire book through these means: "It would be the vehicle for the 'new light' Swedenborg told him [in his vision] to deliver to humanity." [29]

After moving to Manhattan in 1845, "Davis entered a trance day after day for months. He dictated visions of other planets, heaven, angels, afterlife realms, and the spiritual mechanics of the entire universe, all recorded by his minister friend for the pages of a massively swelling book." [30] Since these sessions were actually open to the public, a particularly intrigued journalist by the name of *Edgar Allan Poe* observed Davis' experience of channeled writing (perhaps enviously, since it would make writing much less work!) Being fascinated by Mesmerism, Poe soon would compose one of his most famous short stories, "The Facts in the Case of M Valdemar" (as it was completed later that same year, we conclude Davis was Poe's inspiration). In his fictional account, Poe made his protagonist Valdemar the victim of a Mesmerist who kept him locked in a trance for seven months, until, at the pleading of Valdemar, the Mesmerist 'let his subject go.' Once released from the trance, his body literally and quickly turned into a "liquid mass of loathsome—of detestable putrescence." Most intriguingly, *The Sunday Times of London* would publish Poe's story in 1846 and convey (by omitting any word to the contrary) the account was true (the story entitled, *Mesmerism in America: Astounding and Horrifying Narrative*). [31]

In the account of Davis, Horowitz connects another colorful character mentioned in my earlier book *Decoding Doomsday*: Professor George Bush of New York University (during the 1840s, Bush was Professor of Hebrew, famously predicting the physical reestablishment of Israel in the land of Palestine, 100 years before it happened). This Bush was first cousin, five times removed from the first President Bush. Dr. Bush told the *New York Tribune* in regards to Davis' abilities: "I can solemnly affirm that I have heard him correctly quote the Hebrew language in his lectures and display a knowledge of geology which would have been astonishing in a person of his age, even if he had devoted years to the study." [32]

Like other promoters of spiritualism in America, Davis was committed not only to mysticism but to the social gospel. "For many, the true magic of Davis' message was in its liberalism: sexual and racial parity, religions on equal footing, and a universal faith based on reason." [33] A Universalist religion we might willingly acknowledge; but there was cause some portion of his assertions were made more difficult to swallow—Davis' *source for truth* was a channeled spirit. This entity was a wordy supernatural being eager to have his conversation put down on paper.

Should we be surprised? Hardly. This pattern constitutes standard operating procedure for occultists. Indeed, *channeled material* by definition remains *essential* to spiritualism. It should be no wonder that Andrew Jackson Davis was a medium who should be likened to all leaders of New Age spiritualism (from Helena Blavatsky to Alice Bailey, from Benjamin Crème to Phyllis Schlemmer the 'channel of choice' for THE NINE discussed in *Power Quest, Book Two*). Like them, David penned immense works by taking dictation from spirit entities.

However, the legacy of Andrew Jackson Davis would have greater impact still due to a sophisticated sycophant. His protégé would be one *Henry Steel Olcott*, co-founder of *the Theosophical Society*, traveling companion to *Madame Blavatsky,* and originator of the ideology that found its way back across the pond two decades later. It would be Blavatsky and Olcott's teaching that would infect the minds of many English and Germans, whose penchant for spiritualism was equal to the Americans. As we will see, the chance meeting of these characters heavily influenced Nazi Germany (and therefore, the whole world over). As such, it stands as perhaps the topmost instance of *unfortunate happenstance* known to humankind.

The Birth of Theosophy

Colonel Olcott, as he was also popularly known, grew up a Presbyterian and married the ex-wife of an Episcopal minister. However, despite these Christian leanings, he was fascinated by the occult even as a young lad. At twelve years of age, he took a trip to Poughkeepsie to witness Andrew Jackson Davis make a

Figure 3 - Blavatsky & Olcott, London, 1888

supposedly accurate diagnosis of a sick man in his presence with no more than holding a lock of his hair. This one experience would impact Olcott's life work with far reaching consequences for the next one hundred years of human history. As a youth, Olcott lived the farmer's life in Ohio toiling with relatives. As the Civil War drew near, he obtained an Army commission whereupon he developed a new set of skills that would serve him, and his country well.

> He was placed in charge of a team of auditors and detectives to investigate fraud and forgery among military contractors, and was promoted to staff colonel to lend weight to his investigations. Exposing a racket of fake provisions sales, Olcott saved the Union army enough money for Secretary of War Edwin M. Stanton to write him that his efforts were "as important to the Government as the winning of a battle." His reputation as an investigator grew. When Lincoln was assassinated in 1865, Olcott volunteered his services. Stanton telegraphed him in New York to "come to Washington at once, and bring your force of detectives with you." During the twelve days that John Wilkes Booth remained a fugitive, Olcott and his investigators made the first arrests and interrogations of suspected coconspirators. [34]

After growing rich from government contracts, Olcott became an attorney and began a law practice in New York City. However, he was much more interested in writing than practicing law. But unsatisfied with the standard fare about which he was paid to write (growing bored authoring cultural reviews), "His interest in Spiritualism began to reemerge—especially upon reading press reports of strange happenings at a Vermont homestead." A spirit medium, William Eddy and his brother Horatio, produced a ghost show with Indians in full regalia and featuring personages from afar. "It was here at the Vermont 'ghost farm' that Olcott had a fateful encounter—one that would send tremors not only through his own life but across other continents." [35] Horowitz continues the colorful story:

On the sunny midday of October 14, Olcott stepped onto the Eddy porch to light the cigarette of a new visitor: a strange, heavyset Russian woman with whom he grew quickly enchanted. She showed him flesh wounds she said she had suffered fighting beside the revolutionary hero [Italian] Giuseppe Garibaldi in his campaign to unify Italy; she told tales of travels in exotic lands; and she hinted at far deeper truths about the nature of the spirit world than were revealed to the nightly gawkers at the Eddy home. Olcott was perplexed—and utterly fascinated. The college dropout in him seemed somewhat awed by "the arrival of a Russian lady of distinguished birth and rare educational and natural endowments." He marveled over her tales of "traveling in most of the lands of the Orient, searching for antiquities at the base of the Pyramids, witnessing mysteries of Hindoo [sic] temples, and pushing with an armed escort far into the interior of Africa." [36]

Olcott rented an apartment for himself and his new best friend, Madame Helena Petrovna Blavatsky, at West 47th Street and Eighth Avenue. The New York World jokingly referred to their habitat as the *Lamasery*—referencing the Lamas' monasteries in Tibet. "It was a cramped Neverland of a place where, amid stuffed baboons, Japanese cabinets, jungle murals, mechanical birds, and palm fronds, New York's spiritually adventurous—ranging from inventor Thomas Edison to Major-General Abner Doubleday—huddled to discuss, argue over, and marvel at arcane ideas." [37]

Edison would admit to Olcott and later to a reporter about his experimenting in the occult, specifically looking at the intersection of the technology of the mind with that of mechanical science—an essential element of Theosophy inasmuch as the ideology wasn't just about *knowing* but also about *doing*—specifically physic feats defying logic. (Blavatsky was famous for making things go bump in the night, bringing ringing bells to chorus and achieving other poltergeist-like goings-on). In fact, Edison built one device to test whether the mind could create kinetic force and another to communicate with the dead. Doubleday not only helped develop and promote the then-new sport of *baseball* after a highly reputable career in the military (he lies buried at Arlington National Cemetery), but he contributed to the Theosophy Movement by publishing the first English translation of French magician Eliphas Levi's occult standard *Ritual and Dogma of High Magic,* more commonly known as *Transcendental Magic*. After Olcott and Blavatsky left America heading for India, Doubleday would take over the reins of the American Theosophical Society. *Who says baseball and Buddha don't belong together?*

However, why was Blavatsky in America? HPB [38] indicated that she had been "dispatched to America by a secret order of religious masters—"Mahatmas," or the "Great White Brothers," she would later call them... Her mission was to expose the limits and fallacies of Spiritualism and point the way to higher truths. While she admired the cosmic visions of Andrew Jackson Davis, Blavatsky hinted at secret teachings that the Poughkeepsie Seer and the trance mediums who trailed after him could only begin to guess." [39] All this became firm as fact when,

> One of the turbaned masters materialized before him [Olcott] in their West Side apartment. Addressing Olcott as "Brother Neophyte," one of the Mahatma letters [that Olcott had received, penned in gold ink] directed him to stay at Blavatsky's side and "not let one day pass away without seeing her." He listened—and the two worked together days into nights. They collaborated on Blavatsky's epic-in-the-making, *Isis Unveiled*—a dense, sprawling, and ultimately extraordinary panoply of occult subjects. Blavatsky told of a hidden doctrine that united all the world's ancient religions and cosmic laws but that unknown to materialist science and modern religion... In the typically blunt fashion that made her a favorite of the New York press, Madame Blavatsky publicly declared, "The Theosophical Society means, if it cannot rescue Christians from modern Christianity, at least to aid in saving the 'heathen' from its influence." [Her feelings toward Christianity thus becoming obvious] The *New York Sun*, never wearying of the Russian Madame, dubbed her the "famous heathen of Eighth Avenue." [40]

Indeed, the story of Olcott and Blavatsky could well be summed up as a furtive campaign against Christianity, its strictures, as well as its *exclusivist* doctrines (remember doctrine divides, spiritualism unifies). On the positive side, while in India, Olcott and Blavatsky worked hard for the cause of literacy. On the other hand, in contradistinction to his American background, once in Ceylon (now Sri Lanka), Olcott "spoke in temples and open squares, where he urged youths and their families not to relinquish their Buddhist-monastic tradition and to argue against colonialist missionaries... Olcott used the missionaries' own methods against them: He wrote *A Buddhist Catechism*—still read in Sri Lankan Classrooms today— to codify the native faith as missionaries had the Christian one." [41] His 'do-gooding' gained him great respect, raising money for schools and educational programs. Horowitz further indicates Olcott ignited a Buddhist revival causing the number of Buddhist schools to jump from four to over two hundred. From a religious point of view, *Theosophy comprised how the West saved the East.*

However strange the Theosophical doctrine was to most hard-working Americans (to them, it remained ever so 'hocus pocus' or in the parlance of our day 'off-the-hook'), it wrapped itself in a populist cloak by adding real value to society. In contrast, most religions of the orient are seldom accused of promoting social welfare or undergirding society in general. Nevertheless, the admixture proffered by the odd couple from New York conveyed a social conscience deeply American, earning Theosophy a positive hearing around the globe.

Meanwhile, back in the USA, *Isis Unveiled* was becoming a best seller giving spiritualism a Bible of sorts to satisfy American devotees in their eagerness to grow wise in this new reckoning of reality—an ideology combining *Buddhism, the new discoveries of science, and American individualism.* This three-fold combination was the secret sauce that resurrected a decidedly declining interest in oriental mysticism worldwide and made 'being a mystic' fashionable again.

And if there were any hidden Mahatmas who had sent Blavatsky to America and then with Olcott to India, they might have had reason to be proud of their neophytes on other counts. Back in the United States and Europe, Blavatsky's book *Isis Unveiled* popularized the word occultism and made the concept a matter of passionate interest among artists, authors, and spiritual seekers of the Western world—more than it had been any time since Renaissance scholars had marveled over the magical writings of Greek-Egyptian sage Hermes Trismegistus.

The American Spin on Spiritualism

America was primed for Theosophy because of its previous infatuation with *Transcendentalism*--spurred to life by another man with a similar sounding name: *Alcott* (that is, Amos Bronson Alcott—Louisa May's father of *Little Women* [42] fame) who, along with Ralph Waldo Emerson and Henry David Thoreau plowed the spiritual ground so Theosophical seeds could be sown. [43] Alcott demonstrated great interest in Hermetic matters studying the works of *Egyptian magician* Trismegistus in small groups with his highly intellectual neighbors. Alcott was especially influenced by the literary genius of Emerson (1803-1882) who lived across the road. Horowitz quotes scholar Alvin Boyd Buhn from his 1930 study, *Theosophy*, who asserted the *importance of the connection between Transcendentalism and Theosophy*: "Yet, seriously, without Emerson, Madame Blavatsky could hardly have launched her gospel when she did with equal hope of success." [44]

Figure 4 - The emblem of the Theosophical Society

That is why Blavatsky believed America to be the Mecca of Spiritualism. "The opening created by Transcendentalism made the young nation into a magnet for every kind of spiritual experiment. And like many cultural openings, this one appeared so quickly and dramatically that it could leave observers unsure of what was even occurring." [45]

America's excitement regarding Spiritualism may not be easily appreciated by Americans today. But at the time, many Americans either discarded their Christian faith entirely or amended it dramatically by seeing it through the lens of Theosophy and other spiritualistic cults. *Mystery Babylon was growing strong in American soil.*

It was particularly appealing because of the despairing nature of the times for many. Being able to tap into *the other side* was an enticement that grieving parents could not avoid—and there were many such parents in deep despair. In New York City in 1853, almost 50% of all deaths were children under five years of age. [46] This caused the profession of mediumship to be a method of gainful employment, particularly for women. "In 1850, journalist E. W. Capron counted in Auburn, New York, 'fifty to one hundred' mediums 'in different stages of development,' including those who could induce unseen hands to strum guitars and pound drums." [47] Seeing this musical phenomenon no doubt would have been even more charming than watching the player piano pound the keys at the carnival—both types of playing being (no doubt) about equally mysterious to contemporary audiences.

Horowitz underscores how after 1850 many newspapers and periodicals sprung to life to serve this soaring market. At the peak, those journals almost totaled seventy altogether. His estimates, possibly conservative, suggested that between 10 and 30% of the American population in the latter half of the nineteenth century would have checked the box 'spiritualist' if asked to declare their religion. "Spiritualism was not a regional sensation but a national movement." [48] *America grew obsessed with the paranormal.*

Even President Lincoln and especially his wife Mary Todd were engaged in séances; some of these social events in the Whitehouse included cabinet members where political matters would be posed to the presiding medium. "Once everyone was seated at the table, according to the Gazette's correspondent, Prior Melton, Lincoln gamely pitched political questions to [Charles] Shockle, the 'spirit visitors' who spoke through him, and the two cabinet members, while Mark Todd looked on silently." [49]

After the assassination of the President, Mrs. Lincoln, "so distraught by the death of her husband grew increasingly interested in séances. Ten years after her husband's death, 1875, Mary Todd Lincoln was briefly committed to a sanitorium [sic—committed by her one remaining son Richard], claiming—spuriously—that she was squandering her estate on Spiritualist hoo-ha." [50]

So it is that America produced Theosophy which reinvigorated the spiritualist mindset and spawned many other myths including the 'Black Reich.' Authors Louis Pauwels and Jacques Bergier in their colorful book *The Morning of the Magicians*, Trevor Ravenscroft in his controversial book *The Spear of Destiny*, and other more historically acceptable authors such as Dr. Nicholas Goodricke Clarke (Ph.D. from Oxford—his most famous book, *The Occult Roots of Nazism*) regarded *Theosophy as the key to understanding the preternatural mindset present in Nazi Germany* leading up to World War II.

To finish this section on Theosophy with a flourish, it seems appropriate to underscore America's dramatic influence on Germany with a quotation from author Christopher Hale, who studied the infamous Nazi expeditions to the Himalayas to track down the roots of the Aryan race (which he called, 'Himmler's Crusade,' authoring a book by the same title). He drew these conclusions concerning the effect of Theosophy upon Germany and Europe:

> *The Secret Doctrine* made an especially powerful impression in Germany and Austria. Olcott had even considered moving the Theosophical Society headquarters from India to Germany after the English Society for Psychical Research had exposed Madame Blavatsky as

a fraud (she was caught out writing the letters which she claimed were 'precipitated' by her mahatmas). Some fifty years later, after 1933, Theosophy would become even more popular as Germans were encouraged to turn away from Christianity and embrace faiths that were considered to be more Aryan. For many, *The Secret Doctrine* appeared to reconcile science and belief, nature and myth, and in Germany, it catalyzed a much older intellectual tradition... [51]

All over Europe, and in India itself, theosophy became a cult. Its disciples were not the hungry masses who poured into spiritualist meetings and séances desperately seeking solace; *they were intellectuals, diplomats, philosophers, and even scientists.* United under the Tibetan symbol of the swastika, they infested the salons and laboratories of Europe. As in *The Secret Doctrine* itself, science and occultism lay happily side-by-side in a fetid embrace. [52] [Emphasis added]

Due to the intellectual but arcane offerings of several English literary personages such as Arthur Machen and Sir Edward Bulwer-Lytton, the paranormal penchant of Nazi Germany was not an exclusively Teutonic persuasion. The English historian Houston Stewart Chamberlain was unequaled in his support for the racial superiority and destiny of the German nation. Thus, both the British as well as the Americans provided enormous ideological support for the Third Reich. [53] This influence encompasses only the paranormal influence of Anglo-America on Nazi Germany. It does not take into account the mutual fondness between Adolf Hitler and American businessmen Henry Ford (Ford Motor) and Thomas Watson (IBM) and their crucial contributions to German technology. Nor does it bespeak the vast eugenics leadership America provided to Nazi efforts catalyzing the Holocaust (again, documented thoroughly in *Power Quest, Book Two*). But as to the obsession with the paranormal, the story of Theosophy does not end with World War II.

Theosophy's historical impact transcends the Nazis. If anything, its influence *expands* in the next stage of spiritualism in America: *The New Age Movement.* [54]

With this post-war form of Theosophy, we see less emphasis upon social gospel and more emphasis upon an *eccentric individualist agenda through a sought-after encounter with spirit beings.*

In the latest incarnation of ancient wisdom, the experience of obtaining *personal spiritual power*—a most self-centered focus on spirituality—remains the primary interest. This mystical enchantment today even beckons unsuspecting evangelicals.

Spiritualism and the New Age Movement

Figure 5 - Alice A. Bailey

It is one of the most peculiar themes of latter-day occult philosophy: the insistence that there are a series of 'masters' who live in remote places guiding what happens in our world. These masters take various names. Blavatsky labeled them the *Great White Brotherhood;* hers was an update to her grandfather's 'unknown Superiors.'

This tradition continued with her most important disciple, Alice Ann Bailey (1880-1949, typically nicknamed *AAB* by her followers) claiming they should be addressed as the *Ancient Masters of Wisdom.* Bailey, while born in England, lived most of her life in the United States. Once again, Americans can take pride in (or in the author's case, *despair of*) the influence our native spiritualism has upon the rest of the world.

Like Blavatsky, Bailey channeled her messages, claiming to take telepathic dictation from a supernatural source she identified as *Djwhal Kuhl*, aka DK, the *Tibetan.* She wrote over 20 books, from 1919 to 1949 acting as his agent, commenting to the effect that she didn't always agree with DK, but what he said was exactly what she put down on paper. She knew her supernatural superiors as the *Masters of Wisdom*, of which Jesus was but one (and according to her, *not* the supreme Master). In the *Externalization of the Hierarchy,* perhaps her most famous book, Bailey indicates that the time is soon coming when the 'Hierarchy of Ancient Masters' will appear before all humanity. A prayer given her by DK—known as the *Great Invocation*, calls out to these Masters, imploring them to leave their 'hidden ashrams' behind and live in the cities of the World. For Bailey, the *Christ* translates as a collective title for these various spiritual gurus. The 'Return of the Christ' culminates in *the divine plan* realized through these spirit guides.

Scholars connect the teachings of Bailey and Blavatsky. [55] Strong evidence abounds to support this conclusion. A case in point: when controversy swirled over who would lead Theosophy and the New Age movement, Bailey and her husband, Foster Bailey, a 32nd degree Freemason, led a "Back to Blavatsky" movement to counter her rival Annie Besant. To this day, a debate rages among Theosophists regarding whether Bailey was true to Blavatsky's message.

Nevertheless, Bailey's writings constitute the doctrinal opus of the New Age Movement in America. However, her influence goes well beyond her writings. There are numerous organizations she founded with her husband Foster Bailey including *The Arcane School, The Group of New World Servers,* and *Lucis Trust*, originally known as *Lucifer Trust*. [56] After Alice Bailey died in 1949, Mr. Bailey took over Lucis Trust and continued as chief until his own death in 1977. Some have pointed out the influence of these organizations upon the United Nations. [57]

As with the other oriental religions both past and present, Bailey placed a strong emphasis on transformation, reincarnation, and Karma. Like the Freemasons, she emphasized the mystical powers of *Venus* and *Sirius.* As did Blavatsky, she frequently mentions *Shambala*—the divine seat of power for *Sanat Kumara* who is, according to AAB, the ruler of this world and a focal point for occult power and *eternal life*. [58] Also similar to Blavatsky, Bailey evinced anti-Semitic sentiments, believing the Jews "have bad Karma," blame the Gentiles for all their problems, and "require the best for their children no matter what the cost to others." She talked frequently about "the Jewish Problem" and claimed after World War II, that the occupants of the concentration camps were 80% other races and only 20% Jews. One Rabbi said this of her teachings which opposed Judaism:

> Bailey's plan for a New World Order and her call for "the gradual dissolution—again if in any way possible—of the Orthodox Jewish faith" revealed that "her goal is nothing less than the destruction of Judaism itself... This stereotyped portrayal of Jews is followed by a hackneyed diatribe against the Biblical Hebrews, based upon the 'angry Jehovah' theology of nineteenth-century Protestantism. Jews do not, and never have, worshipped an angry vengeful god..." [59]

New Age proponents, perhaps unwittingly, joined the Manichean heretics declaring the Old Testament God infamously two-faced. [60]

Conclusion: *The Ongoing Impact of Spiritualism*

In the final analysis of spiritualist religion, there appear two different metaphysical schools of thought, metaphorically speaking. First, there are those advancing a slate of affirmations that most wouldn't quibble with. Horowitz identifies such beliefs with these words:

1. Belief that spiritual ideas have therapeutic value.
2. Belief in there is a mind-body connection in our health.
3. Belief that human consciousness is evolving to a higher stage.
4. Belief that thought determines reality.
5. Belief that spiritual comprehension remains available to anyone without pledging allegiance to any one dogmatic religion. [61]

Horowitz suggests these ideas sum up how the occult has influenced America. He concludes: "The encounter between America and occultism resulted in a vast reworking of arcane practices and beliefs from the Old World and the creation of a new spiritual culture. This new culture extolled religious egalitarianism and responded, perhaps more than any other movement in history, to the inner needs and search of the individual." [62] From a popular cultural perspective in America, this summary assessment is essentially true. However, from the standpoint of Christian creeds so influential in other aspects of American life (from our nation's inception and its coming forth), Horowitz's analysis of occult influence, especially in American intellectual history, constitutes a highly insufficient if not innocuous point of view. We see this expressly in the second school of New Age thinkers, especially those who follow the lead of Alice Bailey.

This second school proposes a much more radical and antagonistic agenda. Beware of these spokespersons. Included are Benjamin Crème, David Spangler, Barbara Marx Hubbard, and their disciples in what we used to call the *2012 Movement*. Given their radical antipathy toward American Protestantism as well as their forceful threats for those that do not sing out of their New Age hymnbook, their threats and admonitions should raise the hair on the back of the reader's neck. For example, Hubbard warns, "People will either change or die. That is the choice." [63]

Mel Sanger, an evangelical researcher and contemporary author offers this analysis:

> Unlike the East, where these pagan teachings are familiar, in Western society there is a need to break down traditional monotheistic (and/or atheistic) resistance to them. To ease penetration, New Agers encourage "light encounters," psychic experiences which seem to carry the individual beyond normal consciousness into a new realm of spiritual sensation. Also known as, "a doorway to higher consciousness," the suitably impressed person will be encouraged to seek this

experience on a regular basis. The only way to achieve it, however, is through passivity and a willingness to submit one's mind to outside control of a 'guide.' [64]

There is something especially sinister concerning this segment of the New Age Movement. Like every other spiritualist leader with a theosophical bent, these advisors propose channeling or mediumship as an avenue to advance one's personal spiritual power quest. At a minimum, they encourage grasping *the meaning of life* through seeking ultra-dimensional spiritual forces. But to what are these forces loyal?

David Spangler offers the following less-than-prudent advice:

> The angel of man's evolution, will *(progress us on our)* journey to 'godhood' at the new level, which includes a personal experience of the 'knowledge of good and evil.' New Agers confirm that this knowledge is what Lucifer offered to Eve in the Garden, and it's being offered again today. Only it's been misunderstood, due *to fear inherited from the superstitious Judaic/Christian religion.* Since God has both a good and an evil side [a problematic assumption drawn from Manichaeism], and one cannot attain complete godhood with only one side, Lucifer comes to give us the final gift of wholeness. If we accept it, then he is free and we are free. That is the Luciferic initiation. It is one that many people now, and in the days ahead, will be facing, for it is an initiation into the New Age. [65]

This group, following the lead of Albert Pike (1809-1891), the noted doctrinal authority of Freemasonry and its Universal 'head' late in the nineteenth century, emphasizes the importance of Lucifer, a Luciferic initiation, and the explicit reversal of other-worldly beings from the standpoint of who is the good guy and the bad guy. While most commentators dismiss any suggestion that authentic Freemasonry (let alone the New Age 'A-team' just mentioned) constitutes an anti-Christian religion, *such pundits apparently dismiss or ignore the authoritative remarks regarding Freemasonry's search for Luciferian enlightenment.* So should we, likewise, dismiss what the Freemason authorities say about themselves and avoid taking them at their word? Isn't it relevant that many in Germany in the 1930s dismissed the notion their country soon would be headed down the path to Fascism? Isn't such incredulity increased when we include the possibility such an outcome would be energized by spiritual forces?

Yet, this is exactly the same situation in America today. Who could possibly believe that power players concealed with the nation's most elite families press for hegemony in regards to our national government? Since it is too fantastic to fathom, it must be false. If it is incredulous, it cannot possibly be true. *Au contraire!*

Despite all such reasonable doubt, we must proceed with caution concerning many of the New Age recommendations for spiritual achievement. Indeed, we should especially take into account the form of freedom that Spangler espouses. His 'liberty for life' is normally considered bondage by most psychologists, particularly by those who have engaged with such spiritual forces over the long haul. Likewise, picking up the story from whence we began in this essay—taking drugs to prompt a personal spiritual encounter—promises even stouter cases of addiction and self-destruction. Yes, there is a difference between ritual drug taking and reducing one's stress, just as there is a difference between a hunting rifle and an AK-47. However, no matter the intent, just as the experienced gun owner knows which rifles are legal and which are not, taking hallucinogenic drugs demands even greater reticence. Surely, this guidance for spiritual experience cannot be dismissed by third-parties as harmless counsel merely because it originates from well-meaning New-Age authors attempting to propagate their Universalist philosophy. The stakes for the psychological health of the individual are much too high to imbibe hallucinogens with only an ounce of blind faith as a chaser.

What stands so astounding in 2014: the lessons of America's obsession with the paranormal has reemerged once again, this time within the Evangelical Church. For the church living in Babylon during these last days, the need for discernment has never been greater.

One of the mystical practices in current favor is known as 'Centering Prayer.' What is that? "Centering Prayer is a method of silent prayer that prepares us to receive the gift of contemplative prayer, prayer in which we experience God's presence within us, closer than breathing, closer than thinking, closer than consciousness itself." [66] Centering Prayer comprises one contemplative prayer technique. It draws upon the desire for a deeper spiritual experience such as expressed by the mystics of Christianity (like St. John of the Cross), and even the modern 'Christian Buddhism' of Henry Nouwen (if there can be such a thing). No surprise then: leaders advancing this technique for achieving spiritual growth wander far afield from orthodox Christianity *seeking unity by nullifying doctrinal distinctions.* As hinted earlier, this approach eventually leads to adoption of an intellectually bankrupt Christianity built solely on irrational mysticism and personal encounter. When the nature of God and the unique revelation of His person as revealed in Jesus Christ takes a back seat, spiritual experiences can be achieved which do not connect with the true God—they may range from simply discovering the value of tranquility and inner calm, to the direct experience of other spiritual beings that impinge upon our consciousness and masquerade as the real thing. In this regard, New Age mysticism and so-called Christian mysticism become one and the same. Those caught up in the contemplative movement no doubt chafe at this accusation. *But when doctrinal truth is dismissed or downplayed, there remains little basis for judging one experience valid and another demonic.*

To bring our discussion full circle to the discussion at the outset, taking drugs may enhance the depth of the encounter and the desirable 'learning' (as Graham Hancock advocates), to the 'teachers of mankind.' If the goal is the *depth* of encounter, why not take drugs? Why not encounter any being that demonstrates the efficacy of the supernatural? *As I discuss in Lying Wonders of the Red Planet* (and well-documented by author Peter Levenda, an authority on the occult in America), searching for encounters with spiritual beings constituted the goal of Aleister Crowley and his American follower Kenneth Grant. These two were the most noteworthy purveyors of black magic in the twentieth century through satanic rituals—all to achieve the goal of encountering otherworldly entities.

If *definitive content remains excluded from arbitrating our spiritual encounters*, discernment become an impossible task. As Francis Schaeffer taught us, seeking such spiritual experiences amounts to an irrational 'leap of faith.' Faith becomes 'blind' and we become blinded with no light to guide us.

However, that leads to expanding the story even further which moves us from the *history* of American spiritualism to a dangerous *current emphasis in the evangelical church*. Later in this book, we will add details to the story and underscore the dangers of this purportedly *deeper spirituality* that likely leaves the God of the Bible out of the sought-after encounter altogether.

Notes

---

[1] The movement was so-named by Alice Bailey and her followers in America in the 1930s but became widespread in the 1960s and 70s. I relabeled it the '2012 movement' since it was typically accompanied by predictions for massive change in the consciousness of humankind in the year 2012, when supposedly *the New Age dawned.* Those in occultism believed something significant happened. It was not obvious.

[2] "Shamanism is a range of traditional beliefs and practices that involve the ability to diagnose, cure, and sometimes cause human suffering by traversing the axis mundi and forming a special relationship with, or gaining control over, spirits. Shamans have been credited with the ability to control the weather, divination, the interpretation of dreams, astral projection, and traveling to upper and lower worlds. Shamanistic traditions have existed throughout the world since prehistoric times. Shamanism is based on the premise that the visible world is pervaded by invisible forces or spirits that affect the lives of the living. In contrast to animism and animatism, which any and usually all members of a society practice, shamanism requires specialized knowledge or abilities." See www.crystalinks.com/shamanism.html.

[3] Pinchbeck, *Breaking Open the Head*, 62.

[4] Hancock, Graham, *Supernatural: Meetings with the Ancient Teachers of Mankind* (New York, NY: The Disinformation Company, 2007), 244.

[5] Dictionary.com provides this formal definition of cosmology: It is "the branch of philosophy dealing with the origin and general structure of the universe, with its parts, elements, and laws, and especially with such of its characteristics as space, time, causality, and freedom."

[6] "Cosmology," *Dictionary.com Unabridged*, Random House, Inc., accessed June 30, 2011, http://dictionary.reference.com/browse/cosmology.

[7] Alkaloids such as *dimethyltryptamine*, aka DMT, or *mescaline*, a phenethylamine, both of which are considered *entheogens*, aka psychoactive agents to stir up the "god within us."

[8] Wasson and his wife studied the possibility and concluded that hallucinogens underlie all of humankind's ancient religions. This view is shared by Daniel Pinchbeck and Graham Hancock in the respective books cited here. In other words, to them, God is a magical mushroom, or at least lives within one! "All of our evidence taken together led us many years ago to hazard a bold surmise: was it not probably that, long ago, long before the beginnings of written history, our ancestors had worshipped a divine mushroom?" There is a fungus among us. But this author certainly does not believe it is God (Pinchbeck, *Breaking Open the Head*, 48).

[9] "Turn on, tune in, drop out," *Wikipedia*, last modified March 24, 2011, http://en.wikipedia.org/wiki/Turn_on,_tune_in,_drop_out. It was likely the hysterical nature of Leary and his mad ranting about western culture and the necessity to use hallucinogens to save our souls that "turned off" (rather than on) the American "psyche" to LSD. Today's advocates for the spiritual value of drug-taking blame Leary *for doing far more harm than good* in educating the masses about the personal usefulness of such compounds.

[10] A French phrase meaning reason for existence or "reason for our being."

[11] Levenda, Peter, *Sinister Forces: A Grimoire of American Political Witchcraft*, TrineDay, Waterville, Oregon, 2005, p. 215.

[12] Therefore, not only were the English part-time chefs adding to the occult cauldron of Nazi Fascism, but Americans also contributed to the horrendous evil Himmler and Hitler begat, contributing many influential ideas to the mix.

[13] Ibid., p. 28.

[14] Ibid., p. 33.

[15] Ibid., p. 31.

[16] Ibid., p. 36.

[17] That is, the Neo-Platonists: Bruno, Mirandola, and Agrippa.

[18] Levenda comments on page 40, "As Americans, we have been moving too fast and forgetting too much to realize that we have a unique cultural contribution to make, one that unites religion with mysticism at

the very bedrock of human experience... and then transforms this al-chemical tincture into a political and scientific Philosopher's Stone capable of causing tremendous change in the human psyche." Levenda's celebration of this indiscriminate combination of spiritualism with Christian supernaturalism is, unfortunately, inconsistent with his acknowledgement that many forces are sinister, just as his book title asserts. If so, the need to *distinguish "good from evil"* remains essential for any form of Christian faith that takes the Bible's warnings about spiritualism seriously. Discernment and differentiation go hand in hand as do their opposites: deception and consolidation.

[19] Yes, I do realize that my preceding remarks on Mormonism are quite disparaging. My defense: these facts are historically verified by multiple sources and tell the story of Mormonism's beginnings. Its status today comprises a highly sophisticated religion and bears little resemblance to its origins. However, even this acknowledgement should concern those who are members of the LDS. Christianity's origins are highly regarded and offer positive behavioral models. Not so with Mormonism. In contrast, the most compelling aspects of Mormonism lie in its emulation of the early church *model* and evangelistic methods of historic Christianity. The heterodox teachings of Mormonism, in part are explained due to its spiritualistic, even magical genesis.

[20] Of course, this can be said of most any religion. When any ideology harms the individual and the society, that religion becomes untrustworthy. In fact, members of society are responsible to question the viability of any religion whose affects consistently demonstrate breaking what our Founders called *natural law* which protects basic rights of individuals and communities. We see the recent story of Warren Jeffs and his polygamist cult as a prime example of social evil at full throttle.

[21] Horowitz, Mitch, *Occult America: The Secret History of How Mysticism Shaped Our Nation*, Bantam Books, New York, 2009, p. 3.

[22] Ibid., p. 63.

[23] Ibid., p. 7.

[24] His is an attempt to be non-judgmental or 'politically correct', inasmuch as pluralism attempts to embrace all points of view as

equally valid. I would expect very few who endorse such forms of religion to explain their conduct as *consorting with the devil* even if they were unwittingly practicing pagan methods. I doubt many Shamans see themselves doing anything other than serving the public good—often self-descriptively viewing themselves as caretakers of their community. Those engaged in these practices (channeling, drug taking, holding séances), from their vantage point, aren't seeking to harm—they certainly seek to help and strive to find personal meaning as a byproduct. Value judgments on what they are doing, from a Judeo-Christian perspective are ultimately based upon a comparison to what biblical directives present as proper or improper—indeed, judging occult practices as forbidden and reprehensible. (See Isaiah 47:11-13) In the New Testament, sorcery, also translated witchcraft, stands out as a "sin of the flesh" (See Galatians 5:20) — human beings perform it quite naturally. The New Testament word for witchcraft and sorcery is *pharmakeia,* from which our word *pharmacy* derives. It takes little imagination to see the link between drug usage for spiritual purposes and sorcery as asserted in the Christian Bible. In the hands of the user, such tools seek to empower the individual to manipulate, not just explore, the entities that inhabit this supersensible or preternatural realm. This comprises the most blatant *power quest* of all.

[25] Ibid., p. 64.

[26] Ibid., p. 23. Joseph Smith found his golden plates in western New York, apparently another spiritualist locale. One wonders whether the history in that area before European settlement was especially dark with native occultic activity and devilish rites.

[27] Ibid., pp. 32-33. His letter is taken from *Abnormal Hypnotic Phenomena, Vol. 4: The United States of America* by Allan Angoff, edited by Eric Dingwall (J.& A. Churchill, 1968).

[28] Ibid., p. 33. The Washington letter was drawn by Horowitz from *Franklin in France, Volume II*, by Edward Everett Hale (Roberts Brothers, 1888).

[29] Ibid., p. 36.

[30] Ibid., p. 37.

[31] We might infer tabloid journalism in London had already hit stride 165 years before Rupert Murdoch and the Fox News Corp in 2011 began eaves dropping on voice mail to bolster sensationalism!

[32] Ibid., p. 39. Professor Bush in 1848 published a short book predicting that the nation of Israel would physically become a nation once more. Ironically, 100 years later, Bush was proven a prophet. It is also interesting that Bush eventually left his mainline denominational affiliation and became a follower of Swedenborgism (aka, The New Church), a mystical amalgam of spiritualism and Christianity. It was "founded by the followers of Emmanuel Swedenborg in the late eighteenth century, especially its assertion that Christ is God Himself and not the Son of God, and its reliance upon accounts of mystical appearances of Christ to Swedenborg." (See *www.thefreedictionary.com /Swedenborgism*). Horowitz also points out that the legendary *Johnny Appleseed* was the most famous member of this group! Who would have thunk it?

[33] Ibid., pg. 41.

[34] Ibid., p. 44.

[35] Ibid., p. 44.

[36] Ibid., pp. 44-45.

[37] Ibid., p. 45.

[38] Her nickname, self-imposed and liberally used by her followers.

[39] Ibid., p. 46.

[40] Ibid., p. 47.

[41] Ibid., p. 48.

[42] Louisa May Alcott enjoyed some very special teachers to be sure: "Alcott's early education included lessons from the naturalist Henry David Thoreau. She received the majority of her schooling from her father. She received some instruction also from writers and educators such as Ralph Waldo Emerson, Nathaniel Hawthorne, and Margaret Fuller, who were all family friends. She later described these early years in a newspaper sketch entitled 'Transcendental Wild Oats.'" See *en.wikipedia.org/wiki/ Louisa_May_Alcott*.

[43] On a personal note, I drove by the houses of these famous Americans who lived in Concord, Massachusetts, most every day for five years when commuting from Nashua, New Hampshire into Boston. Additionally, we celebrated my daughters eleventh birthday by having her and her friends dress up in old New England dresses (*Little Women* style) holding a party for them at the Alcott's house, now open to the public. It was a memorable occasion.

[44] Ibid., p. 50.

[45] Ibid., p. 53.

[46] Ibid., p. 55.

[47] Ibid., p.55.

[48] Ibid., p. 57.

[49] Ibid., p. 59. And another story illustrating Lincoln's wit and charm: "When Shockle's spirits did get around to giving their inevitable military advice—through the channeled words of no less than Henry Know, secretary of war to George Washington—Lincoln was unimpressed: 'Well, opinions differ among the saints as well as among the sinners. They don't seem to understand running the machine among the celestials much better than we do. Their talk and advice sounds very much like the talk of my Cabinet.' Lincoln then asked his discomforted cabinet secretaries whether they agreed that the spirits knew little better how to proceed than the mortals—which elicited stammering assurances from Navy Secretary Gideon Welles that, uh, well, sir, he would certainly consider the matter." (Ibid., pp. 60-61).

[50] Ibid., p. 59.

[51] Hale, Christopher, *Himmler's Crusade,* Hoboken, New Jersey: Wiley and Sons, 2003, p. 26.

[52] Hale, op cit., pp. 29-30.

[53] The greatest matter of support from America was in the pseudo-science of eugenics. America led and Germany followed. This historical truth is thoroughly documented in *Power Quest, Book Two.*

[54] Mitch Horowitz's analysis of a number of twentieth century American churches, such as Christian Science, The Unity School,

the Church of Religious Science, and several others may or may not be classified as spiritualist depending upon your definition. I interpret these offshoots of Christianity to be focused on 'mind over matter' and the spirit as an inspirational aspect of reality. Some are more or less orthodox in terms of core Christian doctrines. For instance, Norman Vincent Peale (and the contemporary Robert H. Schuller) might be accused of believing in a less-than-personal God that enhances our lives when we *take charge* and become positive influencers on people and situations around us. However, in my reading of these authors I find no reason to include them amongst spiritualists as there is neither evidence nor promotion of channeling, mediumship, etc., and in the case of Peale and Schuller, there is a strong commitment to core Christian doctrines such as the Deity of Christ, sacrificial atonement, and the like. They were, after all, clergy in the Reformed Church of America, which is ultra-orthodox in many respects. This is not true in the case of Christian Science, Unity, Church of Religious Science, and a very up-to-date flavor of this manner of belief totally without reference to Christian doctrine in the book (and later movie) *The Secret* (Rhonda Byrnes, 2006). These latter belief systems strongly reflect *Gnosticism* (or Manichaeism) and not orthodox Christian affirmations. The teaching of many present day Megachurch pastors are strongly aligned (intentionally or not) with this "blab it and grab it" approach.

[55] See Lewis, James R. and Melton, J. Gordon. *Perspectives on the New Age*. SUNY Press. 1992.

[56] Lucis Trust continues operating today closely associated with the United Nations. Members include such interesting individuals as George Schultz, Henry Kissinger, David Rockefeller, and Paul Volker. This fires the flames of conspiracy to be sure.

[57] Constance Cumby's book, *The Hidden Dangers of the Rainbow: The New Age Movement and our Coming Age of Barbarism,* Shreveport, La.: Huntington House, 1983, was the ground-breaking book critiquing the New Age movement in America.

[58] Shambala was also the city Marco Polo tried to find that contained the fountain of youth, or the "tree of life."

[59] *http://en.wikipedia.org/wiki/Alice_Bailey#cite_note-Gershom-149* .

[60] A recent book by Joseph P. Farrell and Scott D. deHart argue for this interpretation: *Yahweh: the Two-Faced God.* In their book, they blame all monotheistic faiths for a "jihadist mentality." Yahweh is as bad as Allah.

[61] For the record, I would quibble a bit regarding the final three.

[62] Ibid., p. 258.

[63] Hubbard, Barbara Marx, *Happy Birthday Planet Earth*, Ocean Tree Books, 1986, p.32, quoted by Sanger, Mel, Mel, *2012 – The Year of Project Enoch?* Rema Marketing, 2009, Part II, p. 13.

[64] Sanger, Mel, *op. cit.*, Part II, p. 17.

[65] Spangler, David, *Reflections on the Christ*, p.37, quoted by Sanger, op. cit., p. 12, 13.

[66] See http://www.centeringprayer.com/. Centering prayer is also known as contemplative prayer. The complete description:

> This method of prayer is both a relationship with God and a discipline to foster that relationship. Centering Prayer is not meant to replace other kinds of prayer. Rather, it adds depth of meaning to all prayer and facilitates the movement from more active modes of prayer — verbal, mental or affective prayer — into a receptive prayer of resting in God.
>
> Centering Prayer emphasizes prayer as a personal relationship with God and as a movement beyond conversation with Christ to communion with Him. The source of Centering Prayer, as in all methods leading to contemplative prayer, is the Indwelling Trinity: Father, Son, and Holy Spirit. The focus of Centering Prayer is the deepening of our relationship with the living Christ. The effects of Centering Prayer are ecclesial, as the prayer tends to build communities of faith and bond the members together in mutual friendship and love.

To the extent that such prayer is based upon encountering the true personhood of Jesus Christ as disclosed in the Bible, the technique remains valid. When the closeness of the personal relationship forsakes the revealed nature of Jesus Christ as the Second Person of the Trinity, it threatens to become demonic and opens the praying soul to forces other than Jesus Christ.

Evangelicals express a strong personal relationship with the Living God, Jesus Christ, through the Holy Spirit. Through the Holy Spirit, God the Father and the Son dwell within the believer (John 14:26, John 17:23, I John 2:23) Whether or not this experience leads to euphoric feelings or not, the indwelling remains true. When individuals seek to encounter spiritual reality without regard to the God of the Bible, all bets are off. The spiritual realm remains complex and a dangerous place to traverse without a guide. For Jews and Christians, the Bible constitutes the essential "lamp unto our feet."

How the United States Government Helped Nazis Infiltrate the Americas

By S. Douglas Woodward

"[Imperiled Civilization's] efforts have ground the German war machine to fragments. But the struggle has left Europe a liberated yet prostrate land where a demoralized society struggles to survive. These are the fruits of the sinister forces that sit with these defendants in the prisoner's dock... What makes this inquest significant is that these prisoners represent *sinister influences that will lurk in the world long after their bodies have returned to dust."* [Emphasis in original]
Robert Jackson's "Opening Statement" at the Nuremburg Trial

"We knew what we did. It was absolutely necessary that we used every son of a b---- as long as he was an anti-communist."
Harry Rositzke, CIA-Russia expert
[Speaking of German intelligence officer, Reinhard Gehlen]

"There are few archbishops in espionage. He's on our side and that's all that matters. Besides, one needn't ask him to one's club."
Allen Dulles, CIA Director under President Eisenhower

This essay is drawn from *Power Quest, Book Two: The Ascendancy of Antichrist in America.*

IN THIS ESSAY, WE RECAP HOW THE UNITED STATES FACILITATED THE IMMIGRATION OF NAZIS INTO THE AMERICAS. THIS ACCELERATED THE TRANSFORMATION OF AMERICA INTO THE FINAL BABYLON. THE NAZI INFLUENCE, ORIGINALLY INTENDED TO ASSIST IN FIGHTING THE COLD WAR AGAINST THE SOVIET UNION PERSISTS IN OUR POLITICS AND ECONOMY EVEN TODAY.

The Paranoia of Post-War America

LOOKING BACK FIFTY YEARS, IT IS HARD TO IMAGINE THE PARANOIA AMERICA FELT REGARDING THE SOVIET UNION. THE RECORDS OF THE CONFLICT, INCLUDING KEY WITNESSES THAT LIVED through these tense moments, tell us we were within hours of an all-out nuclear war. Jacque Kennedy related her conversation with husband and President John Kennedy during those horrific October days in 1962: "Don't send me anywhere. I want to be with you at the White House. We will die together with the children." [1]

The Cold War has now been over for twenty-three years (dating from the fall of the Berlin Wall, November 9, 1989) with America the clear victor. But at the end of World War II, American leadership believed that we would soon be at war again - this time, with those revolutionary Marxists.[2] This air of suspicion and mindset of mistrust motivated outrageously irrational and sometimes illegal behaviors. Unfortunately, these actions were so horrific that the perpetrators of these activities ensured the cover-up continued for decades afterward. Indeed, what transpired was so contemptible and far-reaching that its legacy and secrecy linger even today. It isn't a question of whether the actions of our governmental leaders were unconstitutional; they were unconscionable. As we delve into the details, the reader will be shocked and horrified. But the truthfulness of these facts now appears no longer open to serious debate.

Why Did We Want the Nazis in America?

In the aftermath of War in Europe, beginning in 1945 and continuing for several years thereafter, certain American leaders determined that the only way to keep our population safe from the threat of Soviet Communism was to employ the intelligence expertise and engineering genius of thousands of Nazis who nearly defeated the Allies. It is generally perceived today that if the war had continued six months longer, the tide would have turned. The Germans had a series of secret weapons that were nearly ready to launch. It has been well documented that the Nazi government had tested the flight of its largest bomber, loaded with what would likely be an atomic weapon bound for New York City. New, more powerful rockets were almost ready to deploy against England. A jet-powered Messerschmitt (the Me-262) was already in service. [3] And as we explored at the outset of *Power Quest, Book Two* it was conceivable the Germans had a completely new order of flying machine not far from its deployment; namely, the *flying saucer*. At the very least, the so-called *Foo-fighters* (little glowing balls of light, full of electro-magnetic energy) were already terrorizing Allied pilots.

However, it wasn't only technology we wanted from the surviving Nazis. We wanted leadership and expertise which shared our fear and loathing for the Communists.

The most famous cooption of German agents was the spy network of Reinhard Gehlen (1902-1979). Gehlen's Nazi organization spied on the Soviets during World War II; aka the Eastern front. Once he was cleared of war crimes (mostly by looking the other way), Gehlen was established in his position by Allen Dulles (1893-1969); his usefulness to U.S. national security was viewed paramount. Dulles, the namesake of the Washington DC International Airport, was the dominating head of the CIA during the 1950s until fired by President Kennedy early in his administration in 1961. Dulles' removal was ostensibly based on the failed *Bay of Pigs* action against Fidel Castro and the CIA's hidden agenda of forcing Kennedy's hand to supply U.S. Air Force air cover for the Cuban invasion (manned by Cuban nationals). This operation was actually planned during the Eisenhower administration. Upon Dulles' removal, Kennedy vehemently told him he would "smash the CIA into a thousand pieces."

Gehlen brought nearly all of his Nazi spy team intact into American intelligence. Given his previous loyalties, Dulles and Gehlen worked out what most would consider an amazing deal for Gehlen: he would provide intelligence on the Soviets to America as long as it was in the mutual interest of the United States AND the *new Germany*. Once West Germany (as it would later be known) had been properly established and was stable, Gehlen's organization would return to German sovereign control. This was an astonishing concession on Dulles' part since Gehlen was intimately tied to the Nazi Hierarchy and had relationships reaching to the highest level. [4]

Dr. Richard Breitman, Professor of History American University and IWG Director of Historical Research, documents the now well-known facts about the amazing employment of Gehlen's spy network after he chronicled the many notorious leaders of the German Reich, some of which had committed numerous nefarious activities and were nonetheless protected from prosecution by the Allies:

> The Nazi War Crimes Disclosure Act of 1998 initiated a search for information in classified American government records about the Holocaust and other war crimes committed by Nazi Germany or its allies. A second target of this law was information about any individuals with Nazi pasts who may have been used as intelligence sources and protected against prosecution after World War II. The Central Intelligence Agency has now [Breitman's article was written in 2000] located and declassified files on a substantial number of individuals suspected of involvement in criminal activity for the Nazi regime or its allies and satellites. In other cases a CIA file on an individual contains evidence about criminal activity by others.
>
> Nineteen CIA "name files' being opened today represent the first significant products of this search within CIA records. One additional CIA file discussed here (the Hitler file) was opened in December 2000... Whose Files Are Now Declassified? The CIA and the IWG have tackled the most prominent individuals first: Adolf Hitler, Klaus Barbie, Adolf Eichmann, Josef Mengele, Heinrich Müller, and Kurt Waldheim. Another fourteen CIA name files involve individuals who served Nazi Germany, survived the war, were suspected of involvement in criminal Nazi or Nazi intelligence activities or had evidence of such activity by others, and came to the attention of American intelligence agencies after May 1945. Nine of the fourteen persons in this second tier had some contact with the West German intelligence organization established by General Reinhard Gehlen, which was initially under the control of the U. S. Army and was taken

over in 1949 by the CIA. Later Gehlen's organization became the *Bundesnachrichtendienst* (BND), West Germany's foreign intelligence agency. [5]

Because he was the master-mind and the most powerful of all U.S. officials driving these decisions, Allen Dulles was the responsible party for this Nazi-American connection. Furthermore, his legacy extends to the obfuscation of the Warren Commission and perhaps, to the heart of the plot to assassinate President Kennedy. This point will be made several times in our study. Whether directly involved in the crime (he had both the *means* through his spy network and the *motive* after being fired from his position), he clearly participated in efforts to hide the truth *after the fact*. But what was his true culpability? As they say, *it's not just the crime - it's the cover-up*.

Joseph Farrell adds these details about the Gehlen organization in his book, *Nazi International*:

> Gehlen was, of course, the German general who was the head of all German military intelligence during the Nazi era for eastern Europe and the Soviet Union, the *Fremde Heere Ost* or "Foreign Armies East", and he was also, of course, the General who secretly negotiated with American OSS station chief in Zurich, Switzerland, Allen Dulles, to turn over to the Americans his entire network so long as the network remained in the day-today operational control of Gehlen himself!
>
> As I have noted in my previous book *The SS Brotherhood of the Bell*, this meant that before President Truman's signature was even dry on the National Security Act of 1947 which created the CIA, its civilian character and charter had already been severely compromised, since almost its entire operational and analytical "Soviet desk" was staffed by a bunch of 'former' Nazis! [6]

Most everyone now knows the story of Reinhard Gehlen; it's beyond dispute. But the details are still subject to debate. Some authors like Farrell propose the key to Gehlen's success was to overstate the Soviet threat flowing additional intelligence funding his direction giving him far greater power. As a result, Gehlen's team of former Nazi spies made the Cold War even more frigid.

America's Nazi Secret

As documented in the Introduction to *Power Quest, Book Two*, attorney and author John Loftus worked for the Justice Department's Office of Special Investigations (OSI) in the 1970s. After leaving his post utterly frustrated, in 1982 he published *America's Nazi Secret* initially *as The Belarus Secret*.

The primary story of the book deals with the horrible tale of how over one million Jews, citizens of Belarus (also known as Byelorussia and 'White Russia') were annihilated by their fellow countrymen. The horrors of their killing were so unspeakable that Adolf Eichmann (1906-1962), the infamous father of 'the final solution' devised a different method for killing Jews. He reasoned that poison gas was far more humane. [7] Based on the murderous methods he witnessed in Belarus to eradicate Jews, he constructed gas chambers. The story of the Belarus monsters which killed over a million Jews constitutes the original crime. However, the primary thrust of Loftus' book relates to the cover-up by Americans who determined the Belarus killers would be useful in our fight against the Soviet Union. It is this cover-up, particularly those facts recently declassified during the last few years, we will study here.

A Highly Credible Source

We should note just how credible Loftus' account is. When the first version was published, it was nominated for a Pulitzer Prize. Mike Wallace, the famous and well-regarded investigative reporter for CBS (who passed away in April 2012), won an Emmy Award for his television presentation based of Loftus' research. Loftus' original book went through five printings and was held as "a seminal work on Holocaust history and on corruption within the American intelligence community." However, his re-release of the book in early 2011 (fattened by myriad documents now declassified by the Departments of State, Justice, Central Intelligence, and military intelligence), is 'invisible' according to Loftus. The author laments no one in the press is eager to review the book, much less wants to take up the subject anymore. It appears that the sleeping dog of U.S. sponsored Nazi incursion into America should continue to enjoy its rest. Loftus doesn't directly clarify whether this reticence is an intentional avoidance of the issue (because the Media has been 'bought' as most authors on this subject assert)—or simply because marketing decisions have been made which presume the American public couldn't care less about our shocking and sordid past.[8] Goodness knows either alternative is equally disturbing.

As a helpful overview and to quickly get the gist of his book, a particular passage concluding his new 2011 edition stands out:

> Over the years, however, the emphasis of the cover-up switched from protecting ongoing operations and agents to protecting the men who had smuggled the Nazis into the United States. [Frank] Wisner [one of Allen Dulles' Deputies at the Department of Justice] and his associates had violated several laws, including the Trading with the Enemy Act, and some statutes of limitations [that] did not run out until 1961, but there were other reasons for the persistence of the cover-up. The major one was the change in the international climate. The Belarus conspiracy was a product of the Cold War and confrontation between the United States and the Soviet Union. Rightly or wrongly, the American people and American policymakers were convinced that Stalin was determined to dominate the world and tailored their actions to meet the perceived threat. Anything that made trouble for the Russians was permissible, including the enlistment of Nazi collaborators. Critics were isolated as appeasers, enemies of the state, or, in the heyday of McCarthyism, "soft on communism." [9]

Loftus measures the extent of America having turned a blind eye to our government's Nazi smuggling, by the fact that Eric

Holder, currently Attorney General for President Obama, eulogized a former Deputy Assistant Attorney General, Mark Richard, in May 2009 at Richard's funeral. Loftus says, "Richard was a despicably evil little man, and one who perpetrated a fraud on Congress, the CIA, Holocaust survivors and WWII veterans. It was he, more than any other, who protected Nazi war criminals living in America and obstructed justice for the victims of the Third Reich." [10] Loftus provides his own post-mortem of Richards:

> Before his death in 2009, Mark Richard commissioned a 600-page classified report in which the Justice Department defended Richard's role in the failed 'hunt' for Nazi war criminals in America. Of the 15,000 Nazi war criminals officially estimated to have lived in America, fewer than one hundred received any form of mild sanction from the Justice Department, and that at a staggering cost of more than a half-million dollars per case. Congress had delivered the money, but Justice never delivered the goods. Nazi hunting may have been the least effective program in Justice Department history. Mark Richard edited the Justice Department document to exonerate himself and to shift the blame to a lower-ranking bureaucrat, Allan Ryan, whom Richard accused of perjury and dishonesty. He devoted an entire chapter of the report to me, claiming that I was an amateur historian who 'exaggerated' things about Nazis working for American intelligence. And then Richard made a fatal mistake. He told the truth, just a bit, but enough to sink his reputation. [11]

Richard had been saying for 30 years that there never was any evidence America had helped smuggle Nazis into America. But in the end he finally admitted, "Well, maybe we did help just a little." This admission opened the door for investigators and researches to peer into the actual documents and see how many Nazis came to America—and how thoroughly the Immigration Service, as well as Departments of Justice and State covered-up the process. We read:

> *Nazi Secrets* was released, without any advance notice to the government, in November 2010 on Veteran's Day (although advance copies were sent to the *New York Times*, which may have provided

an early warning to the Justice Department). That same week, some-one took a copy of Richard's classified report out of the Justice Department safe and leaked it to the *Times*, which broke the story three days later. Now, instead of praising Mark Richard, the *Times* [finally and reluctantly] reported primarily that the Justice Department acknowledged that the U.S. government helped Nazis immigrate and then lied about it. That was the headline that ran all over the country. [12] [Clarification mine]

The New York Times and Its Role in the Cover-up

Loftus indicates not only was the American Government responsible for the Nazi smuggling, but today's bastion of liberal reporting, the *New York Times*, was on the payroll of the Government and had been ever since the 1930s, helping to shape public opinion; eventually downplaying the Nazi infestation during and after it occurred. *The Times* gladly played this role in exchange for 'scoops' from time-to-time on stories U.S. leadership elected to make public. For instance, before World War II, *The Times* frequently published favorable stories on Bolshevism and how well it was faring in bringing new hope to the people of Russia:

> There is no famine or actual starvation nor is there likely to be.
>
> – *New York Times*, Nov. 15, 1931, page 1

> There is no actual starvation or deaths from starvation but there is widespread mortality from diseases due to malnutrition.
>
> – *New York Times*, March 31, 1933, page 13

> You can't make an omelet without breaking eggs.
>
> – *New York Times*, May 14, 1933, page 18

> Any report of a famine in Russia is today an exaggeration or malignant propaganda.
>
> – *New York Times*, August 23, 1933 [13]

One of Loftus' most stupendous revelations: how much our government knew about the holocaust and that the U.S. (and Britain) had such information at the outset of the War. He claims the Americans and the Brits received weekly reports on how many Jews were being killed, but decided that Jewish deaths were acceptable losses in the war effort. In other words, it was a conscious and calculated decision by the Allies that millions of Jewish lives were expendable.

Why would Americans make such a decision? As shocking as it seems to us today, the simple fact is that America's leaders no longer wanted the European Jews to come here. Jews had migrated safely to America for over 100 years. But by the 1920s, Congress refused to alter the immigration quotas to accommodate these immigrants, ultimately sealing their fate. Furthermore, this wasn't purely an economic decision. The anti-Semitic feelings of American leadership were to blame. [14] Additionally, it wasn't just the government that sat on this information. *The NY Times* chose to omit the fact that countless Jews were perishing in Europe under Hitler's policies. Loftus asserts:

> *The New York Times* has a long history of deception by omission. During WWII, the Times omitted numerous reports of Nazi atrocities against Jews, and buried even the smallest mention of what we now call the Holocaust in its back pages. *The Times* has since acknowledged this as a major journalistic failure. During the post-war struggles that lead to the creation of the State of Israel, *Times'* reporting can best be described as neutral or in favor of the Arabs, perhaps because the owner of the paper had publicly declared that if Israel ever became a nation, he would "resign from the Jewish race."[15]

Not only did *The Times* fail to publish the truth about Bolshevism and the Holocaust, according to Loftus, it was a tool for the overthrow of the Allende government in Chile (1973) and the Mossadegh Democracy in Iran earlier (1953) - not to mention (which they didn't) the depth of the clandestine hiring of Nazi intelligence into our intelligence services [16] as described earlier in regards to the Gehlen organization.

Additionally, this artifact of the twentieth century continues to impact our country to this day. Loftus writes of the ongoing collusion between *the Times* and parties within our government which protect *The Muslim Brotherhood*—which has remained the organizing principle in the so-called Arab Spring of 2011 (and continues to this day). Both Justice and *The Times* are unwilling to reveal to the American public that "The Brotherhood" was originally established by the Nazis and employed soon after the war *by the British in an attempt to eliminate Israel early in its history*! Our British brethren chose this terrorist organization in order to protect England's oil interests, aligned as they were with the oil-producing Arab states:

> Someone has shredded the bulk of the CIA's entire file collection on the Muslim Brotherhood. There are only a few press clippings in the file. The *New York Times* continues to publish puff pieces about the wonderful Muslim Brotherhood as an old fashioned anti-colonial political group that may play a modern role in a future Egyptian government. The truth, as this [Loftus'] book reveals, is that the Muslim Brotherhood was the original Arab Nazi movement, working for British intelligence to crush the infant State of Israel. In the 1980s it was hired by American intelligence to recruit the Mujahedeen in Afghanistan, and it is now the parent organization of every Sunni terrorist group in the Middle East. A rather significant omission in *the Times'* coverage of the Muslim Brotherhood, wouldn't you say? [17] [Comment mine—In light of what is happening with ISIS in the Middle East today, who might be behind its training and financing? Saudi Arabia? The CIA? Maybe both?]

Loftus adds further details about how the Muslim Brotherhood was engaged to attack the State of Israel:

> Arab Nazis remain the only segment of the Third Reich that was never punished or even dismantled. After the war, the British Secret Service hired the Ikwahn terrorists, and used them as a fifth column

in an attempt to destroy the infant state of Israel in 1948. When Gamal Nasser and the leftists took over Egypt, they banned this huge army of Arab Nazis now numbering nearly three quarters of a million strong. In the 1950s the same Robber Barons who helped fund and create the original Saudi Ikwahn, convinced their Saudi partners to take them back. The Saudis gladly accepted the Nazi refugees from the Egyptian Ikwahn and gave them citizenship. [18]

As Loftus documents in *America's Nazi Secret* (and in his book, *The Secret War against the Jews*) the anti-Semitic war launched by the Nazis was aided and abetted all told for almost 80 years by the wealthiest British and American elite. Therefore, we cannot rightly conclude Anti-Semitism constitutes an exclusive trait of only select racist (and deceased) Germans. It is a despicable hatred shared by humanity at large. (As I document in *Power Quest, Book Two*, the Eugenics movement which paved the way for the Holocaust was enthusiastically led by American academics and doctors and financed by the Rockefellers_.

History records the Muslim Brotherhood as the parent organization of every subsequent Sunni terrorist group from Hamas to the Palestinian Islamic Jihad. Mohammed Qutb, the brother of the chief Nazi propagandist, was the personal tutor of young Osama bin Laden. Although Congress and the CIA did not know it, the roots of the 9/11 tragedy began in the Eisenhower administration. [19]

Roosevelt's Fight within His Own Administration

When it comes to which political party is to blame for these crimes, Loftus is an equal-opportunity documenter of unlawful activities. He indicates Democrats as well as Republicans are both guilty of importing Nazi war criminals and hiding the truth from public view. "Robber Barons were both Republican and Democrats. In truth they only believed in profit. They were comprised of some of America's wealthiest families, including the Harrimans, Bushes, Rockefellers, DuPonts, and of course, the Dulleses.

It is not an exaggeration to say that they funded both Hitler and Stalin." [20]

In his book, *Nazi International* Farrell asserts the Anglo-American elite decided to test which form of socialism would work best by experimenting with three different types of socialism in the geo-political world: There was FDR's *New Deal* socialism, Joseph Stalin's extreme form of central-government planning (Marxism/Leninism), and German National Socialism (the Nazi Party). Pure Capitalism had become passé.

Having put Bolshevism into power, the internationalist corporate elite soon found itself faced with a problem, namely, that the Soviet Union and its Communist International was serious about expanding communist power—under Soviet auspices—around the world, and particularly into central Europe and Germany. Faced with the possibility of a power bloc centered on Russia and Germany under Communist control, the ability to manipulate and control that bloc—much less oppose it if the need arose—be-

Figure 6 - Nazi International

came quite problematical, if not downright impossible. In short, the balance of power, upon which the larger scheme depended, would have been threatened. Having created the Communist monster, the elite then decided to finance another monster—Nazism—to oppose it. This plan was indeed realistic, since Germany was the only power conceivably in a position to oppose Russia economically and militarily. France and Great Britain simply had neither the muscle nor the geopolitical position to do it, and the United States was ill-disposed to become involved in European affairs. As a result of these considerations, the pattern of international corporate cartel and licensing arrangements between the Western Powers—particularly the United States—and Germany emerged. [21]

Furthermore, to hide their political experiment, wealthy American businessmen [documented in the Introduction to *Power Quest, Book Two*) bought influence in the U.S. and British Government before and after the War. "The money that funded the banks and corporations of the Third Reich came from Wall Street and 'the City,' London, England's financial district and Wall Street equivalent. President Roosevelt knew about it, and so did his Secretary of the Treasury, Henry Morgenthau." [22] But Roosevelt apparently failed to convey to Truman that the real motive for the trial of German bankers at Nuremberg was to finger American and British bankers who were pulling the strings. These actions were buried through the influence of the very wealthy and their attorneys, eventually involving executives within the Department of Justice to assure the truth never came out. Loftus adds:

> Special Assistant Attorney General of the United States closed all of the treason cases in Occupied Germany. Not a single corporate officer ever went to jail for doing business with the Nazis, either in America or the United Kingdom. The Justice Department covered it all up. More than a hundred American traitors were returned home after many profitable years of serving Hitler... Allen Dulles used his position in the OSS to protect himself and his clients from investigation for laundering Nazi funds back to America. [23]

President Roosevelt didn't even trust his own Department of Justice. He kept his Attorney General as well as Vice-President under surveillance for protecting American businessmen who had commercial ties with Hitler's Germany. [24] Additionally, Roosevelt and Churchill worked out a deal where they each would allow the others' intelligence services to spy on their own citizenry so they could both affirm to any future investigators that they weren't using their country's clandestine services for spying on their respective citizenries! Today, we call this technique *plausible deniability*.

Loftus indicates this eventually led Roosevelt to replace his then Vice-President Henry Wallace with Harry Truman who was regarded to be bi-partisan and sensitive to American corporate corruption. What is even more amazing: Roosevelt allowed British Intelligence (the infamous MI6) *to assassinate several pro-Nazi American businessmen in New York City!* This astounding revelation is now public information with newly declassified documents. Loftus states:

> President Roosevelt did not brief Truman on the investigations into Dulles and the Attorney General, both of whom were retained by Truman after Roosevelt's death. What President Truman also did not know was that FDR permitted British assassination teams to murder pro-Nazi American businessmen in New York. Mention of the American-Nazi collaboration and the British assassination teams were censored from the original edition of this book, along with any mention of the Vatican's role in laundering Nazi money back to the American corporate investors. [25]

In the next essay, we will continue the tale of unexpected and shocking assistance provided to the German fascists by the Roman Catholic Church allied with their partner from the past, the monarchies of England. As we will show, this aid has been equally well documented and has also contributed to the transformation of our republic into a State that barely clings to free market economics and religious liberty.

Notes

---

[1] This is a slight paraphrase from an NBC Rock-Center documentary on John F. Kennedy's affair with Mimi Alford, aired in February 2012.

[2] Even at the level of the lower ranking military officers, it was the strong opinion that American soldiers should get home quick, because they would be in another war with the Soviets before too many months had gone by. This was showcased in the movie *Patton* (1970). My father, a lieutenant in Patton's 3rd Army, related this same perspective to me when I was still very young and reaffirmed it again after viewing the movie about old 'Blood and Guts.' (Patton's colorful nickname).

[3] Hitler determined the fate of the ME262 himself. He demanded Messerschmitt make it a blitzbomber although it had been designed as a fighter. Ulrich Brunzel comments that this choice was, "a decision of serious consequences, because the plane had not been designed as a bomber." Continuing on, we read:

> The bomb load alone would make it some 200 kilometers per hour slower and reduce its radius of action accordingly. Both features would make the fighter plane inferior to those of the enemy. Besides, the bomb suspension mechanism had yet to be designed, which meant another delay of at least six months. General Adolf Galland and other experienced flying officers tried to change Hitler's mind, even if, for the time being, in vain. The aircraft was to be redesigned as a blitzbomber. (Brunzel, *Hitler's Treasures and Wonder Weapons*, Heinrich Jung Verlagsgesellschaft mbH, Zella-Mehlis/Meiningen, 1997, pp. 153-155.)

[4] "During the Kennedy Administration, Dulles faced increasing criticism. The pro-American but unpopular regimes in Iran and Guatemala that Dulles had helped put in place were widely regarded as brutal and corrupt.

Several failed assassination plots utilizing CIA-recruited operatives from the Mafia and anti-Castro Cubans directly against Castro undermined the CIA's credibility. The reputation of the agency and its director declined drastically after the Bay of Pigs Invasion fiasco, and Dulles and his staff (including Deputy Director for Plans Richard M. Bissell, Jr. and Deputy Director Charles Cabell) were forced to resign in September 1961.

President Kennedy reportedly said he wanted to "splinter the CIA into a thousand pieces and scatter it into the winds" (reference from a 1966 *NY Times* article). See http://en.wikipedia.org/wiki/Allen_Welsh_Dulles#cite_ref-NY_Times_17-0.

[5] See http://greyfalcon.us/restored/Papercl.htm, p. 1, (3-10-12).

[6] Farrell, Joseph P., *Nazi International,* Adventures Unlimited Press. Kindle Edition, May 1, 2011. Kindle Locations 604-610.

[7] Another key reason to build the gas chambers: the German Military who were at the forefront of murdering Jews were guilt ridden and becoming ineffective in the process. Poison gas wasn't only to make murdering Jews more humane - it was also about 'efficiency' and sheltering the consciences of German soldiers assigned to the macabre task. The critically acclaimed TV Miniseries, *The Winds of War* and *War and Remembrance* (the novels written by Herman Wouk) are graphic and remarkable in showing the details of how this was accomplished in all respects.

[8] Since the recent covers of *Time Magazine*, as showcased in February 2012 by John Stewart on *the Daily Show*, picture international issues dealing with political topics while the U.S. cover for the same editions deals with personal health and entertainment, it is easy to decry American lackadaisical attitudes. Americans are dumbed down and unconcerned.

[9] Loftus, John (2010-11-11). *America's Nazi Secret: An Insider's History* (Kindle Locations 4129-4135). Independent Publishers Group. Kindle Edition.

[10] Loftus, Kindle Locations 163-165.

[11] Loftus, Kindle Locations 175-182.

[12] Loftus, Kindle Locations 188-193.

[13] Loftus, Kindle Locations 265-278.

[14] The infamous anti-Semitic fabricated pamphlet, *The Protocols of the Elders of Zion,* dramatically shaped public opinion in Germany between the two wars. It also impacted public thinking in America. It wasn't helped by the fact that American industrialist Henry Ford reinforced this anti-Semitism through his book, *The International Jew*. For a well written treatment of this subject, see *License to Murder* by Alex Grobman, Noble, OK: Balfour Books, 2011.

[15] Loftus, Kindle Locations 280-285.

[16] Loftus, Kindle Location 279.

[17] Loftus, Kindle Locations 257-263.

[18] Loftus, Kindle Locations 500-504.

[19] Loftus, Kindle Locations 510-512.

[20] Loftus, Kindle Locations 788-790.

[21] Farrell, Joseph P., *Nazi International, op. cit.*, Kindle Locations 1204-1213.

[22] Loftus, *op. cit.*, Kindle Locations 472-474.

[23]Loftus, Kindle Locations 377-382.

[24] Loftus comments:

Roosevelt did not trust either his State Department or Justice Department, he entrusted the post-war probe of American financial collaboration with the Nazis to Henry Morgenthau, his Secretary of the Treasury. Morgenthau initiated *Operation Safehaven*, a program to trace Nazi flight-capital back to the western investors. After Roosevelt's death, Morgenthau was discredited for an anti-German bias at a time when America allegedly needed to rebuild Germany as a bulwark against Russian encroachment. Dulles took over Operation Safehaven, and used it as a cover for OPC's Nazi recruitment. Although Dulles destroyed the Safehaven index, a few of Morgenthau's original files escaped Dulles's shredder, and can be found in the wartime State Department Post Files. For example, in the Switzerland Post files I discovered the Operation Safehaven investigation of Dulles himself, where he was accused of laundering money for the Nazis. My historical novel, *The Witness Tree*, goes into this episode in some detail. The dialogue is fiction, but the story is fact. The Safehaven files were stolen by Eleanor Dulles and given to the Zionist intelligence service. *They then blackmailed Nelson Rockefeller into pressuring the Latin American nations to supply the extra votes in the UN to create the State of Israel."* [Emphasis mine]

Kindle Locations 890-899. America's support for Israel to become a sovereign state was far less enthusiastic than most Americans realize.

[25] Loftus, Kindle Locations 386-389.

Why the Vatican, English Monarchy, and Wall Street Supported the Nazis

By S. Douglas Woodward

"President Roosevelt did not brief Truman on the investigations into Dulles and the Attorney General, both of whom were retained by Truman after Roosevelt's death. What President Truman also did not know was that FDR permitted British assassination teams to murder pro-Nazi American businessmen in New York. Mention of the American-Nazi collaboration and the British assassination teams were censored from the original edition of this book, along with any mention of the Vatican's role in laundering Nazi money back to the American corporate investors."

John Loftus, *America's Nazi Secret*

This essay is drawn from Power Quest, *Book Two: The Ascendancy of Antichrist in America*.

HERE I RECAP WHY THE VATICAN, THE MONARCHY OF ENGLAND, AND MEGA-RICH OF WALL STREET ESTABLISHED NAZI ÉMIGRÉS IN THE NEW WORLD. AN AUTHORITARIAN MENTALITY SOUGHT TO REVERSE THE "AMERICAN EXPERIMENT, "ASSERTING ONLY THE ELITE AND ERUDITE SHOULD ONCE AGAIN RULE. KINGS, PRIESTS, AND **BANKERS** CONSPIRED TO INSTALL A NEW WORLD ORDER.

How the Vatican Helped Hitler Escape to America

THE VATICAN'S ROLE IN FORMING AND MANAGING THE SO-CALLED "RATLINES" MOVING NAZIS TO THE AMERICAS FROM GERMANY BROACHED IN THE PASSAGE ABOVE, COMPRISES YET another intricate and diabolical story. We return to it here to highlight the Vatican's possible role enabling the escape of the most famous of all Nazi fugitives - the Führer himself!

According to Loftus, the Vatican management of the 'ratlines' was headed by the man who would eventually become Pope Paul VI (Giovanni Maria Montini, 1897-1978). Thus, this effort was hardly behind the Pope's back; the 'Pope-to-be' ran the program himself.

As this author was completing this essay [some two years ago], Peter Levenda released a new book entitled, *Ratline: Soviet Spies, Nazi Priests and the Disappearance of Adolf Hitler (2012).* Le-

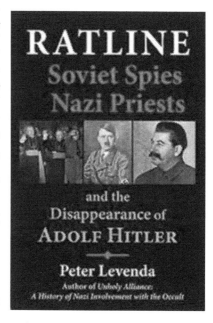

venda's research on the extensiveness of the ratlines, with new proof that they extended all the way to Indonesia, is mesmerizing—mostly because it provides an account of how Hitler may have escaped with his then new wife Eva Braun, first to Salzburg, Austria; then two years later to Argentina, then Brazil, and ultimately to Asia in the early 1950s. The story is much, much too long for inclusion here (and not thoroughly convincing to this author), but the now proven escape route underscores how many important Nazis left Europe due to the Vatican's help.

Figure 7 - Peter Levenda's Ratline

One particular villain central to the story is a Croatian priest, *Monsignor Krunoslav Draganovic.*

> Draganovic was a Croatian priest of the Catholic Church, and a devoted Nazi. His segment of the Ratline was known as the "monastery route" because it used Vatican credentials, Red Cross passports, and monasteries and churches as safe houses along the escape routes. It was a Ratline used by many of the most infamous Nazi war criminals including members of the dreaded SS. [1]

Levenda traces the route of one Georg Anton Pöch to the faraway island of Sumbawa, east of Bali. There he ran a clinic for ten years. His wife was another white foreigner with a German accent. The couple lived together until 1964 when she traveled one-way to Germany never to return again. This trip commenced at the time when the father of Eva Braun was dying. Not long afterwards, the abandoned Pöch remarried an Asian woman in Sumbawa, converted to Islam, and took a Muslim name. He died a few years later in 1970 and was buried in a grave that is reputed by locals to be the grave of Adolf Hitler, mysteriously placed beneath a headstone without birth or death dates engraved. Born in 1889, Hitler would have been 81.

Early in the story, Levenda does a thorough job dispensing with the generally accepted account of Hugh Trevor-Roper and his depiction of Hitler's suicide in the Bunker, April 30, 1945. Levenda points out how little research was in fact done by Trevor-Roper, how few interviews were conducted, how the ones that were smacked of deceit, and how he was hired by British intelligence to write down the account to settle the matter of Hitler's death. In the absence of a body that could be firmly identified (the body was charred beyond recognition) and with a set of 'dental records' which were at best forged, forensic evidence seems especially unconvincing. Add to this situation that Trevor-Roper was also an intelligence agent and doubt intensifies (truth may set the public free as the slogan on the CIA Wall of Honor testifies, but secret agents rarely traffic in the truth). Indeed, if one conclusion seems certain from our study: anytime an intelligence agent records history, there is little chance the truth will find its way into the account. Last but not least: Joseph Stalin emphatically maintained Hitler escaped the Allies and lived on in parts unknown.

Adding fuel to the fire: the skull of Hitler, famously in the possession of Russia for decades, was recently proven not to be that of Hitler - that is, unless Hitler was a woman! An American researcher in 2009 did the DNA tests to prove it wasn't Hitler's head. From *The Daily Mail,* 9-28-09 we read this account:

Adolf Hitler may not have shot himself dead and perhaps did not even die in his bunker, it emerged yesterday. A skull fragment believed for decades to be the Nazi leader's has turned out to be that of a woman under 40 after DNA analysis.

Scientists and historians had long thought it to be conclusive proof that Hitler shot himself in the head after taking a cyanide pill on 30 April 1945 rather than face the ignominy of capture. The piece of skull - complete with bullet hole - had been taken from outside the Fuhrer's bunker by the Russian Army and preserved by Soviet intelligence.

Now the story of Hitler's death will have to rewritten as a mystery - and conspiracy theorists are likely to latch on to the possibility that he may not have died in the bunker at all. The traditional story is that Hitler committed suicide with Eva Braun as the Russians bombarded Berlin.

Although some historians doubted he shot himself and suggested it was Nazi propaganda to make him a hero, the hole in the skull fragment seemed to settle the argument when it was put on display in Moscow in 2000.

But DNA analysis has now been performed on the bone by American researchers.

Where is he? The skull the Soviets found in 1946 is not Adolf Hitler's, tests show. 'We know the skull corresponds to a woman between the ages of 20 and 40,' said University of Connecticut archeologist Nick Bellantoni. 'The bone seemed very thin; male bone tends to be more robust. And the sutures where the skull plates come together seemed to correspond to someone under 40.' Hitler was 56 in April 1945. Mr. Bellantoni flew to Moscow to take DNA swabs at the State Archive and was also shown the bloodstained remains of the bunker sofa on which Hitler and Braun were believed to have killed themselves.

'I had the reference photos the Soviets took of the sofa in 1945 and I was seeing the exact same stains on the fragments of wood and fabric in front of me, so I knew I was working with the real thing,' he said.

His astonishing results have been broadcast in the U.S. in a History Channel documentary titled *Hitler's Escape*. [2]

In essence, Levenda's colorful theory builds upon this assumption: Hitler was doing his best to present evidence of weakness and frailty, sitting in a wheelchair, and showing signs of Parkinson Disease - a state secret unknown to the public concerning Hitler's actual condition by War's end. Levenda surmises:

> Such a stateless person, with no identity documents, would have been an ideal candidate for the International Red Cross passport as well: a travel document that was being issued with somewhat reckless abandon and with little or no supporting identification documentation required... except, in certain cases, identification provided courtesy of the Roman Catholic Church. Such a stateless person would have been able to find another home, anywhere on the planet, particularly if they had the blessing of the Vatican itself. [3]

Levenda cites a lengthy memo from American military sources, dated July 1946, documenting the "monastery route," identifying the major players in this scandal and associating them with the Croats. The memo was declassified in 1985 and was entitled, "Alleged Vatican Protection of Jugoslav [Yugoslav] War Criminals."

> The Croats were largely Catholic, and the idea of a Catholic bulwark against Communism was something that had wide appeal. This concept was mirrored in Argentine fascism, which saw itself and its role in the world in identical terms. Thus it should come as no surprise that there was a natural alliance between the Croats and the Argentines, through the intermediary of churchmen like Draganovic and [Bishop Alois] Hudal. They saw their enemy as Communism, and their natural allies in the fight against the Communists were the Nazis. [4]

Pope Paul XII, Eugenio Pacelli, signed the *Reichsconcordat* (1933) with Germany to guarantee the rights of the Catholic Church there. Many third parties criticize the Pope for doing a deal with the devil. [5] Others suggest that it might have been the best that the Church could have hoped for in the circumstances. However, given that Pope Paul XII was a staunch anti-communist, it isn't a foregone conclusion that the Holy See was simply placating a fascist regime or forced into an "offer he couldn't refuse." The *Concordat* appeared to be a favored course of action. The German Cardinal Faulhaber offered this comment in March, 1933: "After my recent experience in Rome in the highest circles, which I cannot reveal here, I must say that I found, despite everything, a greater tolerance with regard to the new government... Let us meditate on the words of the Holy Father, who in a consistory, without mentioning his name, indicated before the whole world in Adolf Hitler the statesman who first, after the Pope himself, has raised his voice against *Bolshevism*." [6]

Levenda comments:

The Catholic Church has been criticized for this by any number of historians and observers, and the Vatican has usually fought back, insisting that the allegations are without merit. The fact remains, however, that the Nazi war criminals most famous, most wanted, most notorious were protected and aided in their escape by a series of Catholic priests, bishops, and cardinals throughout Europe and North and South America. Whether or not this was "official" policy, it most definitely took place and there was no policy—official or otherwise—to stop it... Photographs of Roman Catholic priests, bishops and cardinals standing shoulder to shoulder with men in the uniforms of the SS or the Ustashe (the fascist Croatian revolutionary movement), giving the "Heil Hitler" salute, could only be construed as evidence of tacit approval. [7]

In a memo dated July 12, 1948 from Paul E. Lyon and Charles Crawford, Special Agents of the CIC (Counter-Intelligence Command) 430th Detachment in Vienna, Subject: "Rat Line from Austria to South America," we see unequivocal proof the U.S. military participated in Draganovic's operation. Levenda cites an extensive portion of the memorandum. Below, I highlight paragraphs 2 and 3:

> 2. Through the Vatican connections of Father Draganovic, Croat, DP Resettlement Chief of the Vatican circle, a tentative agreement was reached to assist in this operation. The agreement consists of simply mutual assistance, i.e., these agents assist persons of interest to Father Draganovic to leave Germany and, in turn, Father Draganovic will assist these agents in obtaining the necessary visas to Argentina, South America, for persons of interest to this Command [the Americans].

> 3. It may be stated that some of the persons of interest to Father Draganovic may be of interest to the Denazification policy of the Allies; however, the persons assisted by Father Draganovic are also of interest to our Russian ally. Therefore, this operation cannot receive any official approval and must be handled with minimum amount of delay and with a minimum amount of general knowledge. [8] [Comment mine]

Clearly, it was seen in America's self-interest to grab the Nazis from the hands of the Communists and place them in America. As we will see from the remainder of the book, this was the very least U.S. leadership hoped would result from helping Nazis westward. Still, we continue to be puzzled regarding why the Vatican would take this course of action and why it, along with our own government, would adopt such a dangerous and deleterious policy. *Herein rests one of history's most profound demonstrations of* **realpolitik**.

Returning to the words of John Loftus, he suggests we should realize the Vatican's motive was two-fold: first, it was due to a legacy of anti-Semitism (hatred to "the Christ killers"); and more perfidiously, because the British and Americans promised the Vatican rights to the life-insurance benefits paid for Jewish deaths due to the Holocaust! Loftus makes this final judgment:

> The financial rot inside the Justice Department that began before WWII has never been cleansed. It has given corporate America

a continuing source of blackmail against the career bureaucrats at DOJ who participated in the original Nazi cover-up... DOJ continues to be involved in the modern sequels, the Arab Nazi recruitment of the 9/11 terrorist groups, an inadvertent result of American oil company manipulation of DOJ and State. The Old Nazis are the New Nazis, their old evil still bottled in the same old barrels of oil. [9]

Other New Stories of the Great Escape

Jerome R. Corsi released a short exposé on the same topic in the spring of 2014, *Hunting Hitler: New Scientific Evidence that Hitler Escaped Nazi Germany.* Corsi's book provides some new information but stands as only a cursory treatment. He reinforces much of the material provided by others such as Peter Levenda and John Loftus. On more than one occasion, Corsi quotes Levenda who noted that some of the most notorious of all Nazis escaped Nuremburg and were aided in their escape in no small part by the Catholic Church. The names include Josef Mengele (the *Angel of Death*), Klaus Barbie (the *Butcher of Lyon*), and Adolf Eichmann, who was the point man for the Holocaust. Eichmann was eventually captured by Israel's *Mossad* through a daring "snatch and grab" in Argentina during 1960 that angered most diplomatic corps across the Americas and Europe, since Israel did not get prior approval of the Argentinians, ignoring their sovereignty. (Of course, Argentina would never extradite Eichmann to Israel and would tip him off if it learned the Mossad was in hot pursuit).

Corsi confirms the role of the American Intelligence in aiding the Nazis and especially in the person of Allen Dulles. Corsi provides this particular bit of insight:

> Particularly controversial were the negotiations code-named "Operation Sunrise," or alternatively, "Operation Crossword," in which Allen Dulles played a direct role in negotiating the surrender of German forces in northern Italy. In this 2011 book, *Nazis on the Run: How Hitler's Henchmen Fled Justice*, historian Gerald Stein-

acher argues that the decision to exclude the Soviets from the Operation Sunrise negotiations with the Germans marked the beginning of the Cold War. Steinacher notes that suspicions remain that Dulles offered protection to the German Wehrmacht and SS officers in Italy during the Operation Sunrise negotiations. "Dulles had certain interests in common with the German generals and, therefore, reportedly intervened on behalf of his German partners in Sunrise," Steinacher wrote. "All SS Officers who took part in the operations managed to escape serious punishment after the war. Some were later hired by US intelligence services; other were able to flee to South America or start new careers as private businessmen." [10]

Corsi also points out that a number of books written in Spanish that have never been translated into English make a stalwart case for Hitler's post-war residence there. These books document Hitler's escape and the fact he was never identified or seriously pursued by the Allies (despite early U.S. Navy intelligence reports of his clandestine arrival). First, a trilogy was written by Abel Basti, an Argentinian journalist. His three books were *Bariloche Nazi: Historical Sites Related to National Socialism* (2004), *Hitler in Argentina* (2006), and *Hitler's Escape: The Proof of Hitler's Escape to Argentina* (2010). Corsi also indicates Italian journalist Patrick Burnside wrote a book in 2000 (*The Escape of Hitler: His Invisible Life in Argentina and the Connections with Evita and Perón*) from which documentary director/producer Noam Shalev produced a film, "Hitler in Argentina." (Corsi derives this information from an article by Michael Santo in the Dec. 31, 2012 edition of *The Examiner*, "New 'Hitler in Argentina' documentary claims Hitler did not die in 1945." My search, however, of the IMDB database did not yield confirmation of this film's existence).

Corsi falls short, however, of including more than one or two references to a now more popular and revered work, *Grey Wolf: The Escape of Adolf Hitler* (2011) written by historian Simon Dunstan and journalist Gerrard Williams. Their book digs deep into personal accounts of the individuals surrounding the last days in Hitler's Bunker and how Hitler, Eva Braun, and their beloved dog

Blondi, escaped first through a network of underground tunnels from Hitler's Bunker office, a series of short airplane trips, and finally a lengthy voyage aboard a German U-Boat (U-530) arriving in Patagonia at the southern tip of Argentina on or about July 11, 1945. From there, Hitler joined many other Germans expatriates settling on the shores of Nahuel Hapi Lake, an area resembling the Alps, at San Carlos de Bariloche, a small town in the Province of Rio Negro. Dunstan and Williams supply a staggering level of detail and tell a spell-binding story. Most of all, their extensive eye-witness accounts provide believable details and add plausibility to the tale of Hitler's escape. Interested readers could do worse than reading *Grey Wolf* carefully with an open mind. Given the substantial number of books taking up the subject and their general consensus that Hitler settled in Argentina, Levenda's theory has subsequently lost its luster. Still, the argument that Hitler did not commit suicide has gained substantial credibility over the past ten years. Since the body claimed to be that of Adolf Hitler appeared to be that of a double, the ashes of the body were never identified as Hitler, and the skull of Hitler held for years by the Russians proved to be that of a woman (DNA methods for identification proving this), we see that yet another important and dramatic aspect of history has been practically nullified, apparently the product of Allied propaganda.

The Royals and Their Support for the Nazis

In Book One of *Power Quest*, this author went into detail documenting the fascinating story of Rudolf Hess and his ill-fated "peace mission" to England. As related there, this extravagant excursion was part of a conspiracy between Hitler and at least a portion of the British Battenberg family [11] hoping to reinstate King George VI and the Royalty into total control of the country—ending the republican form of British government from the Glorious Revolution to today. From the viewpoint of King George (father of Queen Elizabeth II), Prime Minister Winston Churchill simply *had to go*. (We must recall that the English monarchy was in fact essentially German and had been for several generations.)

Loftus brings additional information to the story adding substantial support to the theory of Hess' trip and the monarchical conspiracy at its root.

One prominent royal, Edward, Duke of Windsor, had actually served as King before he was forced to abdicate. He claimed that he left the throne "to marry the woman I love" [the American Wallace Simpson]. The truth, however, is that SIS [MI6] wire tappers had made phonograph recordings of the Duke of Windsor making pre-war deals with Hitler's Ambassador to the Court of Saint James. Even after his abdication, Windsor was regarded by J. Edgar Hoover as "such a dangerous Nazi agent" that he was kept under Allied surveillance throughout the war.

Figure 8 - King George VI

Forced to abdicate in December 1936, Edward and his American wife, Wallace Simpson, toured Germany in 1937. During his visit with Hitler, the dictator promised to restore him to the throne of England as its first fascist King. As his part of the bargain, it was said, Edward successfully betrayed the entire plan of the Maginot line to the Third Reich. British intelligence interceded just as Edward and Wallace were preparing to flee neutral Spain for Germany. They were seized and interned in the Bahamas for the duration of the war. At Churchill's request to President Eisenhower, the *Justice Department covered up the Windsor secret until I stumbled across the files in the Attorney General's Top Secret vault* [Emphasis mine] [12]

But not only did the long-departed British royals (the father and uncle of Queen Elizabeth) deserved to be flayed for their treason, so did many American bankers. Loftus' boss, another true hero, one Walter J. Rockler, discovered a German document during his Nazi war criminal investigations (Rockler and Loftus were the good guys at the Justice Department) that listed *thirteen American banks who were actively working with the Third Reich during the War!* After Rockler's investigative unit was shut down, Rockler kept the list safely hidden so it wouldn't be shredded by those at Justice who were paid to cover the tracks of the duplicitous American bankers they served. [13]

Loftus informs his readers that one of the most important government officials who was responsible for hiding the truth and overseeing dossier shredding was one Henry Kissinger. His role, which has been documented convincingly in Loftus' book, will no doubt never be broadcast by the media. This disclosure would surely upset the apple cart! Kissinger remains something of an American hero and a frequent guest analyst on most media Sunday Morning talk shows.

As to the details: we learn Kissinger, a staunch anti-communist whose reputation included a willingness to consider the use of the atomic bomb against the Soviets (implying a strong resemblance to the featured character in the 1964 movie, *Dr. Strangelove),*[14] was mentored by Allen Dulles while Dulles was still running one of the (mere!) twenty-two American intelligence groups active immediately following World War II (and before the CIA was officially instituted into law through the National Security Act of 1947). Dulles headed the Office of Policy Coordination (OPC), a cover for an intelligence operation resident within the State Department, where:

> Kissinger was recruited as a professional spy for Dulles shortly after the end of the war in Europe. Although there is no evidence that he personally recruited Nazis, Kissinger ran the intelligence file room where records of Nazi recruitment were kept. He then transferred to Harvard where he specialized in recruiting foreign students for espionage. Later he worked for Dulles during the glory days of Office of Policy Coordination (OPC). He was hired as a consultant for a private

group known as Operations Research Office, which planned to use former Nazis as agents behind Russian lines in the event of World War III. Mention of Kissinger's classified work was censored from the original manuscript of this book [*The Belarus Secret*]. [15]

The Politics of Profit

To reiterate, while the primary story in Loftus' book concerns the atrocities and the cover-up of perhaps the worst Nazi collaborators of all—community and political leaders of Belarus aka Byelorussia—the real story regards the Americans and the British elite who set patriotism aside for profit. As noted, Loftus claims the Department of Justice was in the pocket of the wealthy American elite *even as early as at the end of World War I.* He indicates the then Attorney General was a 'bagman' for the Robber Barons during the Versailles Treaty (1919), agreeing to finance the war reparations saddled on Germany, while putting the next generation of Germans into such deep debt there would be no earthly method to repay—except, of course, by gaining control of German patents and retaining pledged corporate stock controlled by the Swiss. "The German currency might have been almost worthless, but German stock was priceless. By the 1930s, Germany had achieved a near-monopoly on high-tech industries, particularly in chemical processes."[16]

Hitler's finance minister, Hjalmar Horace Greeley Schacht, was born in Brooklyn and understood the financing gambits of Wall Street having himself been a player on Wall Street. Although Hitler banned foreign ownership of German companies at the outset of his first achieving political authority:

> In response, the Robber Barons used their influence to pass the Swiss Bank Secrecy Act of 1933. The Wall Street crowd secretly owned the stocks of the Swiss Banks, which owned the stocks of the German banks, which owned the stocks of the German companies. Hitler never knew how the Thyssens and their Wall Street investors kept their financial control intact, at least not until after war broke

out, and the Wall Street ties to a third group of terrorists was finally exposed [the Bolsheviks]. [17]

To protect their earlier Russian investments (which originated in a scheme to harvest the market opportunity in post-Czarist Russia), the Robber Barons created an industrial park in eastern Poland, near the Russian border, near vast fields of coal. Canals were also built to facilitate Russian materials barging from this park to the Vistula River. The Polish province was known as Silesia and the coal company became known as the *Silesian American Coal Company.* Who may we ask was at the helm? As mentioned earlier, it included the Harrimans (Democrats) with Prescott Bush (Republican) sitting on the Board of Directors. As Loftus chides, "Funding Hitler was a bi-partisan event." And as this author has asserted previously, when it comes to understanding what happens in the world, *political parties are far less important than most Americans realize.* Had Hitler not taken over Poland, the industrial park would have become a "profit center for Wall Street." As it turns out, Hitler had a far more despicable purpose for the convenient shipping of massive loads of railcars and barges to the area. The Polish know the town as *Oswiecim*; the Germans called it, *Auschwitz.* So it is that American industrialists literally laid the tracks facilitating the Holocaust.

Loftus passes this summary judgment:

> The bottom line is that for nearly a century, segments of the U.S. Justice Department and the State Department have been running a foreign policy directly at odds with orders of the Presidents and contrary to the knowledge and consent of Congress and the American people. This ongoing bureaucratic mutiny has nothing to do with ideology – they funded the Nazis and the Bolsheviks alike. There was no conspiracy, just a large number of separate Wall Street sharks swimming in parallel lines towards their bleeding victims. It was all about the money. [18]

Joseph Farrell provides a similar assessment:

Between 1927, only two years after the founding of the cartel, and the outbreak of the war in 1939, I.G. Farben had more than doubled in size. The Wall Street financiers who made the loans to Hermann Schmitz [head of I.G. Farben] to form this cartel had indeed created a monster, and that monster, in turn, was not proving to be as cooperative or pliable as they might have wished: [Quoting Anthony Sutton, *Wall Street and the Rise of Hitler*] "By 1939 I.G. acquired a participation and managerial influence in some 380 other German firms and over 500 foreign firms. The Farben Empire owned its own coal mines, its own electric power plants, iron and steel units, banks, research units, and numerous commercial enterprises. There were over 2,000 cartel agreements between I.G. and foreign firms – including Standard Oil of New Jersey, DuPont, Alcoa, Dow Chemical, and others in the United States. The full story of I.G. Farben and its world-wide activities before World War II can never be known, as key German records were destroyed in 1945 in anticipation of Allied victory." [19]

In fact, as Farrell later points out, the liquidation of I.G. Farben as a result of its involvement in World War II was *finally concluded only relatively recently, in 2003 to be precise, almost 60 years after the war ended.* The wheels of justice do grind slowly indeed.

Conclusion—The Cover-up Continues

Although many years have passed, secrets of Nazi infiltration into America have been carefully protected despite numerous congressional investigations (all of which were sabotaged, cut short due to controversy, or abandoned when—in their case—Rockler and Loftus got too close to the truth). Loftus provides considerable detail to document how resolute our government remains to this day, stubbornly refusing to admit the truth. Unfortunately for Loftus, this sad story has essentially become his biography:

For the next several decades, I all but abandoned my legal career to collect and declassify the hidden files that should have been made public before the 1985 Congressional Hearings. Like Rockler, I wanted to protect as much as I could from the Justice Department shredder. Nearly thirty years later, almost two thirds of the Nazi files have been legally declassified by the U.S. Government. The remaining one third, of course, awaits British permission before the CIA can release them to Congress. Many Americans, particularly veterans and victims of the Holocaust, will be astounded to learn that the Justice Department itself was directly behind the Nazi cover-up, betraying the sacrifice and suffering of both. Although the CIA does not realize it (they never do), their own newly declassified records released to the National Archives in 2009 make a very convincing case that it is the Justice Department which has been lying through its teeth to Congress. Included in these newly declassified files is the CIA's account of how my superiors at the Justice Department, lobbied Congress to cancel the 1985 hearings... [Hearings which would have exposed much of the truth's suppression about the Nazi infestation of America - comment mine] [20]

For the interested reader, in the bulk of his book Loftus provides the horrid story of the Belarus atrocities. Moreover, he articulates the intricate details demonstrating the full extent of the *political machinations of the Justice and State Department bureaucrats up to the present day*. Neither story supplies encouraging reading.

However, our primary interest here was more than just to establish the facts surrounding Nazi political intrigue which still impacts American bureaucracy and other governments of our world today. In the preceding essay, I explained how the spiritualism shared between the Germans, English and Americans built an preternatural worldview that led to the great atrocities of World War II (which is documented much more thoroughly in *Power Quest, Book One)* and *how the scientific know-how* developed by Nazi Germany (and in some cases mutually developed with the United States—the focus of *Power Quest, Book Two),* radically transformed crucial segments of the United States government and the moral fabric of our society—to our detriment.

In the next essay, we will draw out the economic and political implications advanced by the historical developments of the twentieth century, leading to the elimination of sovereignty in the twenty-first century for the principal nation states of the western world.

While Babylon may be centered in one great megalopolis and one primary national entity that comprises the "hammer of the whole earth" (Jeremiah 50:23) and through which "every merchant must buy or sell" (Revelation 18:11, 15), it does not stand alone. It comprises a world system ready to be commandeered by that final great leader the Bible calls *antichrist*.

Notes

---

[1] Levenda, Peter, Ratline: *Soviet Spies, Nazi Priests, and the Disappearance of Adolph Hitler*, Lake Worth, FL, Ibis Press, 2012, p. 17.

[2] Http://www.dailymail.co.uk/news/article-1216455/Hitlers-skull-really-womans-Fresh-doubts-death-tests-bullet-hole.html#ixzz1rsLrg1Hb.

[3] *Ibid.*, p. 65.

[4] *Ibid.*, p. 69.

[5] Quoting from Edmund Paris, *The Secret History of the Jesuits*:

"Mr. Joseph Rovan, Catholic writer, comments on the diplomatic agreement between the Vatican and the Nazi Reich on the 8th of July 1933: 'The Concordat brought to the national-socialist government, considered nearly everywhere to be made up of usurpers, if not brigands, the seal of an agreement with the oldest international power (the Vatican). In a way, it was the equivalent of a diploma of international honorability.'" (Page 13).

And later, Paris quotes a Michael Schmaus, professor at the Faculty of Theology in Munich, who wrote:

"'Empire and church is a series of writings which should help the building up of the third Reich as it unites a national-socialist State to Catholic-Christianity...The national-socialist movement is the most vigorous and massive protest against the spirit of the 19th and 20th centuries... The idea of a people of one blood is the focal point of its teachings and all Catholics who obey the instructions of the German bishops will have to admit that this is so... The laws of national-socialism and those of the Catholic Church have the same aim...'" (Page 15).

[6] See http://en.wikipedia.org/wiki/Reichskonkordat#cite_note-15.

[7] Levenda, *op. cit.*, *Ratlines*, pp. 70-71.

[8] *Ibid.*, p. 72

[9] Loftus, Kindle Locations 404-407.

[10] Corsi, R. Jerome, Ph.D., *Hunting Hitler: New Scientific Evidence That Hitler Escaped Nazi Germany*, New York: Skyhorse Publishing, (2014), p. 101.

[11] The name of Battenberg was changed in 1917 to Mountbatten and later altered to Mountbatten-Windsor, Elizabeth and Phillip known as the House of Windsor, while the Duke of York, Elizabeth's third child, uses the surname Mountbatten-Windsor. This was a ruse to cloak their German heritage.

Mountbatten is the family name originally adopted by a branch of the Battenberg family due to rising anti-German sentiment among the British public during World War I. On 14 July 1917, Prince Louis of Battenberg ("Prince Louis I") assumed the surname Mountbatten (having rejected an alternative translation, "Battenhill") for himself and his descendants, and was created Marquess of Milford Haven.[2] The name is an Anglicization of the German Battenberg, a small town in Hesse. The title of count of Battenberg, later prince of Battenberg, was granted to a morganatic branch of the House of Hesse-Darmstadt in the mid-19th century.

Prince Philip of Greece and Denmark, the consort of now-Queen Elizabeth II, adopted the surname of Mountbatten from his mother's family in 1947, although he is a member of the House of Schleswig-Holstein-Sonderburg-Glücksburg by patrilineal descent. (See http://en.wikipedia.org/wiki/Mountbatten.)

[12] Loftus, Kindle Locations 421-430.

[13] Rockler assigned Loftus to head the Belarus investigation in 1979 in the Office of Special Investigations (OSI).

[14] It is often pointed out that Kissinger bears a strong resemblance to the aggressive and enigmatic Dr. Strangelove in the movie by the same title (starring Peter Sellers as several characters in the movie). Strangelove proposes to the President to "use the bomb" after actor George C. Scott, playing the head of the Joint Chiefs (General Buck Turgidson), has rationalized American civilian loses "as 50-60% tops."

There were a number of startling coincidences from the film associated with the Kennedy assassination. According to a summary of the making of the film in the Wikipedia article on the movie *Dr. Strange-love*, we read these amazing details:

> A first test screening of the film was scheduled for November 22, 1963, the day of the John F. Kennedy assassination. The film was just weeks from its scheduled premiere, but because of the assassination the release was delayed until late January 1964, as it was felt that the public was in no mood for such a film any sooner.
>
> One line by Slim Pickens – "a fella could have a pretty good weekend in Dallas with all that stuff" – was dubbed to change "Dallas" to "Vegas," Dallas being the city where Kennedy was killed. The original reference to Dallas survives in some foreign language-dubbed versions of the film, including the French release.
>
> The assassination also serves as another possible reason why the pie-fight scene was cut. In the scene General Turgidson exclaims, "Gentle-men! Our gallant young president has been struck down in his prime!" after Muffley takes a pie in the face. Editor Anthony Harvey states that "[the scene] would have stayed, except that Columbia Pictures were horrified, and thought it would offend the president's family." See http://en.wikipedia.org/wiki/Dr._Strangelove.

[15] Loftus, Kindle Locations 462-466.

[16] Loftus, Kindle Locations 531-533.

[17] Loftus, Kindle Locations 546-549.

[18] Loftus, Kindle Locations 810-814.

[19] Farrell, *Nazi International*, Kindle Locations 1307-1315.

[20] Loftus, *op. cit.*, Kindle Locations 667

Democratic Globalism and the Fate of America

By Douglas W. Krieger and S. Douglas Woodward

"The United States is the only country in the world that is in a position to initiate a change in the world order, to replace the Washington consensus with a global open society. To do so, we must abandon the unthinking pursuit of narrow self-interest and give some thought to the future of humanity."

George Soros

This essay is drawn from *The Final Babylon: America and the Coming of Antichrist*

IN THIS ESSAY, WE EXPLORE THE RATIONALE USED TO JUSTIFY THE ELIMINATION OF NATIONAL SOVEREIGNTY AND INDIVIDUAL LIBERTY. ALSO COVERED: THE INABILITY OF THE EVANGELICAL CHURCH TO STAND AGAINST THE RISING TIDE DUE TO ITS UNBALANCED FOCUS ON PERSONAL SUCCESS AND PROSPERITY.

The World's Commercial Empire

FOR THE MOMENT, THE UNITED STATES OF AMERICA HIDES HER TALONS. HOWEVER, WHEN SPURRED TO ACTION AND DRIVEN TO SPREAD ITS AWESOME WINGS AS A REGAL WARNING TO ITS foes, no rival state, no toothless tiger (such as the UN), and no global consortium like the G8 or the G20 can stare down the daunting hulk appropriately symbolized by the American eagle.

The plain truth: No entity other than the U.S.A. can impose its will politically or commercially upon the entire planet—no nation exists which is beyond our conquest—in the highly unlikely event we decided to take that uncharacteristic action.

For the time being, America languishes as the sleeping giant swatting at flies. Twenty-five years ago, the economic disintegration and political demise of the former Soviet Union, established America as the world's sole superpower. This hegemonic empire found herself the inheritor of all that exemplifies civilization, be it the high cultural expression of Egypt, the seductions of Sodom, the international trading empire of Phoenicia, the mystical religion of Babylon, and especially the organizational and military genius of *Pax Romana.*

From a military standpoint, America remains unchallenged by any singular State or alliance of nations. It has been termed the 'New Roman Empire' some ten years ago by Russia's President Vladimir Putin when unilateral and pre-emptive action against Iraq was pending. The United States determined it would 'go it alone,' if necessary, without UN, French, German (or at that time, Russian) support. Furthermore, America has arguably waged her wars for the past half-century, more out of national interest than to diminish the threat of communism or to support the establishment of democratic freedoms in spite of socialist foes. When it came to halting racially or religiously-based genocide, America chose to engage in the former Yugoslavia, but abstained in Rwanda and the Congo.

Indeed, the 'Bush Doctrine' or any other canonized foreign policy has never been consistently applied based solely upon its core premises. Today's hesitant 'lead from behind' military policy of selective intervention by the Obama administration, supplies a smoke screen to cloak the real party responsible to ensure success in selected military acts. America remains the only power that has the capacity to make good on its political commitments, with the unquestioned military muscle necessary to carry the day.

This bashfully spoken and seldom overtly discussed agenda—protecting American interests, freed from self-righteous rationalizations—has grown more pronounced over the past decade as the U.S. fought against 'state-sponsored' terrorism, certainly in Iraq, but even in the war fought in Afghanistan. America's overtly aggressive policy hides cloaked in the guise of what has been termed abstrusely as *geo-political realism* (a perspective suggesting we cannot wage war solely on the premise of differing values). Ultimately, it is motivated by what syndicated columnist Dr. Charles Krauthammer calls 'Democratic Globalism'—a term coined during his speech given before the American Enterprise Institute, Annual Public Policy Research Council in February 2004, when he received the Irving Krystal Award for public policy.

America's True Golden Rule

Democratic Globalism (according to Krauthammer) is the realpolitik of the twenty-first century and the only resolution to the 'anti-realism' and self-hate of 'liberal internationalism' historically embraced by the Democratic Party, which sees no redeeming attributes within the self-centered 'national interest' policies of geopolitical realism. Because of its idealistic stance, liberal internationalism could be accused of undermining American national interests, since it argues military action exists as an option only when the moral high ground is available to justify interventionist policy (viz., the Carter Doctrine). What makes matters even more complicated: The 'moral high ground' argument has been proven vacuous over the past three years when trying to pick sides in the so-called *Arab Spring*. We once supposed it was easy to invoke the military option out of 'humanitarian intervention' when helpless peoples were being massacred (e.g., Bosnia, Somalia, and to some extent, Libya). Furthermore, defining a foe as a supporter of terrorism, and in the case of Saddam Hussein, a threat to use WMD, certainly made the two longest wars in American history more palatable to the public. During the past year (2013), our inability to take action in Syria to protect its innocent populace stands as a prime example of how difficult a decision we have even when the moral choice is 'obvious' but what best serves our national interests is not. For in the end, all 'Syrian options' may provoke equally unsavory outcomes; probably doing little more than sucking enemies Iran and Hezbollah (in Lebanon) deeper into the Middle East sinkhole—

along with (unnecessarily) nettling the Russians. As we write this essay, the relationship between presidents Obama and Putin is hardly cordial with 'NSA secret leaker' Edward Snowden (aka Benedict Arnold or Daniel Ellsberg—you pick) receiving safe transit through Russia on his way to Cuba and then Ecuador (where he actually winds up nobody knows—although Russia seems to be his last stop).

Looking at the superficial if not misdirected statements made by politicians today, this ignores the real motives and activities driving geo-politics. Both political parties march to the same beat when it comes to leading the country down the path to Democratic Globalism. The goal of creating a *New World Order,* called for by President George Bush the Elder (exactly 11 years before 9/11) [1] smacked of the centuries' old idealistic ambitions of Rosicrucians, Freemasons, and even occult groups like the Theosophists. For the time being, devious tactics seem apparent in the form of a multi-tiered program of mass media disinformation conjoined with possible false flag operations designed to frighten the American public. But to what end? Many voices claim our 'masters' seek greater control of the masses to benefit the common good. Apparently, such covert programs would decrease resistance to world government among most Americans who recognize the erosion of national sovereignty will easily lead to the diminishment of personal liberty while failing to achieve the goal of world peace.

The challenge for those who see what is really happening: *Speak too loudly—one is branded and ridiculed as a conspiracy theorist; speak too softly—one only helps the program further its goals.* For unofficial disclosures, made by unaccredited sources, can do little more than *initiate* the masses to what game is truly afoot. Such ineffectual insurgency against the masterminds of the globalist agenda may even be an element taken into account by such planners—an implicit tactic bespeaking their wicked genius. The policies of self-interest defining America's globalists in the only recently unipolar world are very pragmatic as American notions often are. Despite waving olive branches, reigning Democrats such as the present Obama Administration (or the Clinton Administration for that matter) are as willing to engage in military action as were the previous Republican regimes of Bush the Elder and the Younger. Indeed, new revelations surfaced daily in the summer of 2013 regarding domestic surveillance against American citizens, the IRS used as a hit-squad to take down political adversaries, and the press targeted by the White House when it gets out of line (such as wire-tapping the Associate Press and the paranoid surveillance of Fox News' chief Washington Bureau correspondent, James Rosen). These admissions only prove that fascist-like tactics are not the exclusive property of so-called political conservatives drunk with power. Consequently, realism and economic self-interest, though decried by the Democrats, has captured the 'nobility' within our current administration. Despite a self-righteous sense of imbuement to the calling of a higher mission, unwarranted self-confidence in its academic acumen, and implicitly holding to a stirring ethical mandate 'to look out for all humanity,' pre-emptive wars are still fought and justified in the name of domestic tranquility.

Remember Ben Franklin's counsel: *Those willing to sacrifice freedom in the name of greater security are worthy of neither.*

Furthermore, listening to the definitive capitalist and über-financial manipulator George Soros patronize the rest of us by chiding how we must give a damn about the rest of humanity (as the justification for why nationalism is so 'yesterday'), makes Democratic Globalist motives seem positively messianic. Listen to the arrogance of Soros:

> "The United States is the only country in the world that is in a position to initiate a change in the world order, to replace the Washington consensus with a global open society. To do so, we must abandon the unthinking pursuit of narrow self-interest and give some thought to the future of humanity." [2]

The Globalist, if you believe his or her polemic, seeks to spread 'democratic freedoms' through which Western civilization hopes to tame barbaric, medieval religions of the Middle East (and eradicate their meager remains here in the West—the goal of Nietzsche's Übermensch—remnants which survive in too few Judeo-Christian institutions opposing such Orwellian *doubletalk*). [3]

That is where Krauthammer's analysis goes awry. Our current policy of throwing our economic weight around is not the first time the world has witnessed a mostly *commercial* approach to controlling geo-politics. According to Krauthammer, we are NOT an empire in the classical sense of the term—we are the 'custodian of the international system.'

True enough. We are not now exclusively, nor will we be forever bound by what Krauthammer calls 'the Gulliver Effect' in which the colossus can only strain at the tethers strapped upon him by international midget organizations like the UN, planning convocations such as the G8, G20, Bilderbergers, Trilateral Commission, or Council on Foreign Relations. America talks a good game about fully cooperating with other industrialized nations, but when the going gets tough, you can bet we will continue to act in our own self-interest (witness our years of *Quantitative Easing* at the expense of those who hold our debt), [4] even while our leaders campaign for more expansive world government as an opiate to assuage our allies who dare to believe we mean what we say.

Commerce as Empire

Nevertheless, it is true that today's export-driven economies, massive population flows, regional conflicts over resources (like energy, food, and water), and post-9/11 terrorist activities have made American isolationism fall from favor, leaving Democratic Globalism standing as our much preferred normal course. Woodrow Wilson (rest his soul) with his failed League of Nations, and the Rockefeller Family—the impetus behind the United Nations (Kabuki

Theater at its best)—should be feeling especially vindicated. For the moment, America exists shackled by chains of its own making (not forged by the *People* of course, but by both our known and unknown leaders who spend most of their time creating fetters that befit us). Again according to Krauthammer, we are a benign, reluctant but powerful COMMERCIAL REPUBLIC, not an exploitive and land-hungry empire of antiquity or recent colonialism. And, as the custodian of the international system, we will decide cooperatively but nonetheless out of our own self-interest, when, where and how to defeat our most immediate problem; that is, *Islamic fundamentalism*, which has not only made terrorism an every-day threat to Western cultures, but has radically altered the status quo in the Middle East. The ongoing so-called *Arab Spring* (now in its fourth season) [5] promises many more surprises! Also related, but downplayed for the time being, are the Islamic demographics which tell us Muslims are steadily breeding themselves, as is their right, into majority status across Europe. This back-burner revolution further threatens the dominance of white, Anglo-Saxon, German, and French elites used to manning the helm of their respective governments—as these mushrooming Muslim communities alter societal standards and mores, steadfastly choosing cultural 'non-assimilation,' at the expense of what's left of Europe's individual national identities.

Then there is our less-than-above-board absconding with the earth's oil reserves in the name of Democratic Globalism—which rewards our Commercial Republic's participation in the Middle East pseudo-democratization process—simultaneously gaining the spoils of territorial conquest as we embed ourselves through building local military bases. *Pax Americana's* military stands ready—in the name of fighting global terrorism—and will remain on indefinitely as a threat to crush those not aligned with U.S. economic priorities.

No doubt the patriotically sensitive reply: "Surely America's economic policies (euphemistically entitled 'Free or Fair Trade') are *not* designed to enslave the bodies and souls of men, *nor* to heap up wealth for the Merchants of the Earth who are made rich through trading with America (Revelation 18:3)? No, America stands for freedom! Of course we mean well in supporting liberty, free enterprise, and espousing democracy—we are, after all, the last and best hope for the world! *American Exceptionalism* is the presupposition that guarantees we will do right in the world!" Bible believing readers might note how such talk is idolatrous to the core. Only Jesus saves.

These ideals comprise what all Americans hope would be true of our conduct. On the other hand, all real patriots not frightened by objective analysis, do keep watch—questioning whether we genuinely attain such worthy aspirations. Unfortunately, those seeking the truth find we are not always so pure in our policies or exemplary in our accomplishments.

Krauthammer's claim that our Commercial Republic bears no resemblance to any empire of the past is actually not accurate. True, America is not Rome, not Medo-Persia, and not Charlemagne's Holy Roman Empire. Neither is she a colonizing empire like the British, French, Dutch, or, less recently, the Spanish. Certainly there remain only faint comparisons to the excesses of the Nazis or the Communists—(although the admissions of the last few weeks during the summer of 2013 are disturbing portents, perhaps of worse things to come). [6] The unipolar world of American hegemony (i.e., with many 'foreign benefactors' of her Commercial Republic), does share an uncanny resemblance to another international trading empire some 3,000 years ago—the *Phoenicians;* aka the biblical Kingdom of *Tyre and Sidon* which ruled the Mediterranean and beyond, navigating beyond the Pillars of Hercules, perhaps even into the New World.

In fact, this ancient commercial empire whose influence continues even today in matters of alphabets, religious notions, and commercial inventions (trading pacts, the tool of money, and the creation of commodity markets to manage and create wealth), seems a perfect archetype of America. Given the typology of biblical connections between Tyre, Tarshish, and Babylon explored by these authors in the work THE FINAL BABYLON, America appears particularly well-suited for a run at prophetic fulfillment as the full-fledged Babylon of the Last Days. In fact, the question for the true patriot to consider is this: Does the United States of America fit the description of Tyre and of Babylon that flagrantly summons the Bible's condemnation? Does our nation serve as the powerbase for the enemies of the LORD? Could the leader of our country someday become the Antichrist of the Bible in spirit or in reality? Just how close are we today to realizing this dark fate—and how much do the actors on stage and producers behind the scenes really direct the play? Have they made the Faustian bargain? Have they sold their soul (and our fate) to Mephistopheles?

Who Are the True Agents of Change?

In the name of global democratization, America appears eager to go forth 'conquering and to conquer' mounted upon a white horse (often seen by eschatology scholars as an allusion to the Antichrist—see Revelation Chapter 4, and the figure of the 'Warrior Beast' of Revelation 13:4, "*Who is like unto the beast? Who is able to make war with him?*"). In the name of liberty (often duplicitously), we seek to extend freedom to all peoples oppressed by political despots that destroy human freedom and misguided religious tyrants which sacrifice the dignity of human thinking. The planet awaits its greatest hour, so we are told, and preemptive aggression (rather, 'liberation') by the world's only unipolar power still lurks as a viable alternative 'on the table.' The third world is almost guaranteed to remain in third place, even though it may be allowed to enjoy some measure of progress to mitigate intermittent threats of social unrest (we surely must keep it around since it remains a cheap source of goods and services, not to mention essential raw materials to fuel our consumerism and militarism).

However, the truth is this: the only thing worse than being irreparably harmed to the point of no recovery (forever put into the place of debtor), is to be made to believe 'it's for your country's own good'—although the facts show that only the top-tier of the third-world social order receives the lion's share of economic and social benefit. Despite all claims to the contrary, despite the good-intentions of classic liberalism as well as today's Democratic Globalism, the truth still remains: *"The poor you have with you always"* (Matthew 26:11). Moreover, at least classic liberalism actually thought it could make a difference. Claims made by Democratic Globalists seem at best hypocritical and at worse mere propaganda which misleads not only the common people, but the globalists themselves. For even the smartest people in the room characteristically believe their own hype.

In contrast to the do-gooder mythology paraded before us by American policies and politicians, Democratic Globalism purveys *a policy of greed, not goodwill*—masquerading as a moral crusade of good over evil, freedom over autocracy, and prosperity over poverty. Hence, this covertly commercial resolve demands an interior motivation that can only be supplied by that which espouses, defines, and provides moral covering for "Gulliver in his modern-day travels." Arise, the *new indefatigable Right*—now inclusive of prosperity motivated evangelical southern Protestants mustered by megachurch celebrity pastors, and coupled with pro-family elements inside religious America—e.g., Mormons, Fundamentalists, and Conservative Catholics—too often blithely in league with secular humanist neocons, especially those that glisten with the trappings of success.

Together, these strange bedfellows unwittingly salute the aggressive policies of an imperial Presidency (more often in Republican garb than Democratic), determined to rid the world of terrorism—and in so doing, quietly rule the earth. Nowadays, both religious and profane conservatives are greeted with enthusiasm by the oft corrupted corporate benefactors—the same ones who guzzle petroleum profits and corner other commodities secured through an aggressive policy of economic domination—i.e., 'corporatism.' Such control is secured through the threat of military conquest and subjugation, all under the banners of global democratization, freedom, liberty, and the elimination of 'evil doers' from the planet.

Mission Accomplished!

Consequently, over the past twenty-five-plus years, today's Robber Barons have galvanized the new American vision of a milder, less militant, and more internationally responsible U.S.A. through media complicity, corporate public relations, and financial subterfuge of the world economic system (how does one justify 'bankster derivatives' anyway?) while capturing the so-called 'value's voter' in America. The old 'Moral Majority'—so important to America's 'swing to the right' during the era of Ronald Reagan—has been superseded by a milder, less militant evangelicalism. In other words, evangelicals today are much less evangelistic, while they are also generally *disengaged* in serious public discourse and remain outright *disenchanted* with politics.

You ask, "What is their highest priority in our day?" All too often, evangelicals, especially their leadership, seek to secure a place in society's status quo or get their names on the list of 'up and comers'—both of which are dedicated to the principle of preserving the Old Republic. In so doing—they have masterfully hijacked the moral high ground by claiming uprightness remains on their side; and, in the process, performed a 'Jesus makeover,' dressing him in commercial clothing. Additionally, they have quieted Jesus' biblically authentic threat to disguised secular hedonism/consumerism *. . . even as he chastens Christians obsessed more with plenty than piety!*

Author Krieger was raised in a home where Mom and Dad were stalwart Democrats. Not only were they died-in-the-donkey-hide democrats, they would vote for a jackass if the democrats ran one for President—and that may have happened on more than one occasion! He remembers when Mom came home from *Blue Diamond* (an association of almond growers) in Sacramento and told him she was fired for trying to organize a union—which to this day does not exist there! *A labor union*—that is right—Krieger's mom was a *Teamster* and proud of it. Nonetheless, their faith was steeped in social values that mirror those of the conservative right today. And yet, the 'Dems' embraced a socialist activism that got real peculiar as far as Mom and scores of other old-fashioned democrats were concerned. So what happened? Go to Wichita, Omaha, or Oklahoma City and find out if you do not know. What's happening for blue collar workers happens all over the nation as the working class struggles and the middle class dissolves. The only ones that cannot figure it out are leaders of the Democratic Party. Today, it is not so much the workers who support the Democratic Party—it is those who would rather not work much at all!

Workers of the world unite! And while you are at it, oust the Democrats who, if the truth be known, could care less about those who have to work for a living! They just want votes.

On the flip side of the political spectrum, the conservative Republican 'caucus' has now been thoroughly replaced by the 'neo-Con' ideology. Not that its tenets are clearly understood. The traditional symbol of the GOP (that funky elephant) ought to be exchanged for an overweight chimeric 'El-if-I-know' because our confusion (and everyone else's) regarding what Republicans stand for today has finally reached its own sort of convoluted singularity! The meaning of being a Republican is lost on us! All we know is that Republicans are more business-friendly than Democrats and they seem to realize that taxing the common man and the not-so-rich cannot be justified under the mantra of 'paying their fair share' to grow Government—not to mention paying IRS employees bigger bonuses to gouge the rest of us (and most recently, attack those that stand in their way).

Indeed, the 'old generation' of Republican Party leadership remains, stifling the possibility that something fresh and magical could bring new life into the Republic. The 'old guard' still guards. They continue on as prominent leaders of the choicest metropolitan country clubs. They are diluted only by the newly rich socio-religious conservatives—many of whom are white refugees from the disenfranchised 'Solid South.' Most evangelicals today filtering into Republican leadership, predictably promote the newly updated *Gospel of Prosperity* (preached so positively by most megachurch meta-ministers); and, *ipso facto*, there stand but few amongst us rank and file evangelical patrons of the Constitution that remain willing to challenge the pseudo-spiritual ideology forged by these (1) imbued with new 'churchly values', or (2) inculcated by the age-old corporate American values tying liberty to profitability. The classic heresy has arisen again: *judging one's standing with God by the amount of money in the bank.* Paul lays it on the line: Such *"people [are] of corrupt mind, who have been robbed of the truth and who think that godliness is a means to financial gain."* (I Timothy 6:5, NIV) And yet, I Timothy 6:6 teaches *"godliness . . . is a means of great gain"* if combined with *contentment*! (From the verse of singer/songwriter Sheryl Crow: "It's not getting what you want, it's wanting what you got!"—although some would point out Dale Carnegie said it first).

> ⁶*But godliness **with contentment** is great gain.*
>
> ⁷*For we brought nothing into this world, and it is certain we can carry nothing out.*
>
> ⁸*And having food and raiment let us be therewith content.*
>
> ⁹*But they that will be rich fall into temptation and a snare, and into many foolish and hurtful lusts, which drown men in destruction and perdition.*
>
> ¹⁰*For the **love of money** is the root of all evil: which while some coveted after, they have erred from the faith, and pierced themselves through with many sorrows. (I Timothy 6:6-10)*

Moreover, the new and improved evangelicalism of the American Right [7] has not really leavened the loaf of the Republican Party as much as providing a superficial moral casing to cover-up the old Republican stereotype of the 'too-rich-to-care.' In the end, both Democrats and Republicans alike, whether actively or passively, support efforts which subjugate both U.S. and world economies under plutocrat control. Remember the Golden Rule: *He who has the gold makes the rules*—which the rest must heed.

For those of us who cherish the liberties we hold as unalienable and given by our Creator, we fear we are now much too enfeebled to turn back the momentum of Democratic Globalism espoused implicitly by leaders of both political parties. We will pay for our failure to heed Thomas Jefferson's sage advice (although usually ascribed to George Washington) [8] to steer clear of European politics and 'entangling alliances.' We have allowed ourselves to become the pawns of the financial elite who muster our military to make the world safe for their globalist economic advantage. As the capitalist head of corporate media giant said to his lunatic newscaster in the 1976 movie *Network (paraphrasing a bit),* "There is no U.S., England, France, Soviet Union, or Saudi Arabia . . . There is only IBM, Xerox, Coca-Cola, Aramco, and GM!" [9] While oversimplified, the point was plain enough. *Fascism* (where governments and big corporations join hands to build an unbeatable economy) stands as the guiding principle of *Democratic Globalism*. Whereas America was the champion of free markets and the rights of persons to engage in profitable enterprise, for too long we have allowed big corporate power players to impose monopolies upon us at home and abroad, established in the name of free markets and fair trade! Simply put: *Politicians are in the tank with Corporate America because corporate contributions keep politicians in power*. And any real measure of power seems to corrupt absolutely. [10]

George Washington, Thomas Jefferson, and John Adams must be turning over in their graves. This is not the America they intended and we once knew—and *neither* political party stands willing to speak in a sincere attempt to stop the madness!

In the name of freedom and liberty, of democracy and the banishment of terrorism and tyranny, we have unwittingly committed ourselves and our posterity to march to the beat of a drum played by the nameless elite and mercurial financial henchmen who manipulate markets, while their spokespersons preach about what is best for the middle-class and the down-trodden. Excuse us if we find all such talk egregiously disingenuous. Indeed, Supreme Court Justice Ruth Bader Ginsberg recently stated that Egypt should not look to the *outdated* U.S. Constitution in drafting a new constitution, but to that of South Africa—since our Constitution is now so flexibly interpreted that it can suit any political regime once ascended to the Oval Office.

Conclusion

Perhaps we have been too critical of our fellow Americans, too disdainful of our nation's missteps. Therefore, we should make sure the reader understands *we find fault in all manner of economic or political theory supposing utopia can be achieved in this life.*

For the United States, even when operating outside its Constitutional moorings, has assuredly *not* cornered the market on failure to detect ones' own shortcomings.

A 'crusade against evil' in the mind of either of the last two administrations—launched against the genuinely evil forces of global terrorism and their byzantine networks—reminds us of communism's stupidity, a generation ago when Brezhnev proclaimed the USSR's overt military acts were wholly justified, as its 'sacred internationalist duty' to thwart all attempts to subvert socialism's glorious experiment across the globe. Communists are proven just as myopic as the rest of us! This does not mean true terrorists are not real enemies—they are. But it points out how easily our leaders can disguise sheep in wolf's clothing with no more than a home-made costume. Just because our President says someone is our enemy does not mean they really are.

Likewise, the Fascists can easily demonstrate their blindness as regards Über-National Socialist shortcomings. Joseph Goebbels' famous dictum holds true today: to tell a believable lie, the bigger the whopper the better—while a cacophony of lies works well too!

Speaking of Joseph Goebbels, hear what Hitler's False Prophet authorized, via Dr. Otto Dietrich, when he declared not all that many years ago in the name of freedom:

> Herein lies the secret of the indestructibility of Adolph Hitler and his work—the guarantee that the road he has taken cannot be altered. For it is no longer the man Adolph Hitler, it is no longer his works and no longer the road he has taken that expresses itself in him. It is the German nation itself that expresses itself in him. In him the nation loves itself; in him it follows its most secret desires, in him its most daring thoughts become reality. Every single person feels this and because of it Adolph Hitler is a stranger to no one, and no one is a stranger to the Führer. Workers and farmers speak with him; Nobel Prize winners and artists, warriors and dreamers, happy men and despairing men speak with him, and each and every one hears his own language, he understands and is understood in return. Everything is natural and self-evident, and no one is shy before this great man. No one is ordered to follow. No one is courted, but everyone is called, just as one would be called by his own conscience. He has no choice but to follow, should he not want to be guilty and unhappy in his own heart. Thus, what must happen happens voluntarily, and *no nation on the face of this earth has more freedom than the Germans.* [11]

Pretzel logic notwithstanding (Goebbels was the Minister of Propaganda after all), a simple faith in a larger-than-life leader appeals to most of us. Although the speech of an orator may diminish the complexities of political realities (and not just the discourse), the fact remains no simple solution exists to the challenge of human government. Our current President, a master orator with an appealing persona, has certainly learned this lesson well even as his poll numbers are in steady decline. His speech at the Brandenburg Gate in Berlin (June, 2013) demonstrated that the enthusiasm and promise he presented there just five years ago has unquestionably waned in the minds of Europeans too. [12] Now the question arises for many: "Is there any there *there*?"

There remains little question that overly-exuberant nationalism led to deadly wars throughout Europe for hundreds upon hundreds of years finally culminating in two world wars primarily begun there. [13] Doubtlessly, this grim reality played no small part in motivating miscreant creations like the United Nations, Trilateral Commission, and Council on Foreign Relations. Democratic Globalism promises something even worse: A monolithic government, too unwieldy to manage on a world-wide basis, with no checks and balances to mitigate against the risk that a totalitarian leader will take the helm (a transformation happening today in America as witnessed through the inaction of the Congressional Oversight Committees and their customary ineffectual effort to get to the bottom of any major scandal). The tyranny of the committee will cry out for the efficiency of a dictator, whether benevolent or not so much. For as much as the plutocrats and elitists seek a government ruled *by reason alone* (in the spirit of the *Illuminati*—there, we said it!), unfettered by the tyranny of monarchs, priests, and religious authority—their self-centered agenda of the rich, by the rich, and for the rich—in reality promises little relief from despotism, less freedom for the individual, and diminished economic benefit for the masses.

This is why the Bible warns that what we label the USA (*The Final Babylon)* awaits humanity in the days leading up to the Apocalypse—before the Messiah comes literally to win the day and usher in the Kingdom of God. Babylon will be a regime financed by the "kings of the earth" who give over their authority to a solitary figure known in Christian "literalists" parlance as "The Antichrist." Consequently, we believe a dystopian, not utopian, future approaches in the days that lie just ahead. *We believe that Democratic Globalism, the current guiding light of our world leaders, will be the ideological means by which this dystopian destiny comes to pass.*

Allow us to pose a number of questions (i.e., equivocations). Can we regroup in time? Can we recover an authentic form of republicanism? Can we wrest control from hidden factions and plutocrats who deride U.S. sovereignty? Can we return to a government which considers our Constitution sacrosanct? Can we be rescued from the fate Democratic Globalism intends for us? Can we long endure the culture of 'intolerance' for all but the 'tolerant'—aka those who stand for nothing (but fall for anything)?

NO! The opportunity for equivocations is a luxury we no longer can afford. We are flat out of time—the storm has broken full upon us and it will only grow worse. The ascendancy of Antichrist in America is unstoppable—we affirm the Scripture speaks this word to THIS generation—we must stop trying to reform, to fix, to beautify this sow's ear into a silk purse. The system is not salvageable. We agree that "evil triumphs when good men do nothing" (Edmund Burke)—but we are not advocating doing nothing. Instead, we must remember the evangelical imperative. We must call this generation, our generation; to repent before it is too late. From our vantage point, we have arrived at the prophetically inevitable; the game (forgive the metaphor) has come down to the final 'two minutes'—maybe the final seconds.

We are solemnly called to testify in the street of that Great City. *Babylon the Great* stands condemned—she now unknowingly awaits her judgment. The sooner the Church comes to terms with the fact we are in the final throes of Messianic birth pangs, the better. The Titanic is sinking—stop rearranging the deck chairs! The message could not be clearer: NOW HEAR THIS! GET INTO THE LIFEBOATS!

As Christians, we must stop accommodating 'Sodom and Egypt' where "our Lord was crucified"—Democratic Globalism inserts itself into every corner of our lives. Despite its pernicious presence, the Church worries over political correctness and acquiesces to Babylon's end-times fornications. The apostasy of the last days, the 'falling away from the faith' surrounds us.

The late intellectual Francis A. Schaeffer in his thought-provoking work on Jeremiah, *Death in the City,* asked, "In what has been called a post-Christian world, what should be our perspective and how should we function as individuals, as institutions, as orthodox Christians, and as those who claim to be Bible-believing?" [14] His answer: "The church in our generation needs reformation, revival, and constructive revolution." But he did not say revolt against 'the government.' Frankly, *there isn't time to reform our government, there is only time to awaken the Church to the reality of our situation and sound the refrain of repentance.* Revolution is not the answer for the government or the Church.

The call is an urgent one: In the words of our Savior and his forerunner 'Elijah'—"*Repent for the Kingdom of Heaven is at hand!*" (Matthew 3:2)

True saints in these last days are called to prophesy, to testify, to decry THE FINAL BABYLON'S falsehoods and sins. It is time: Don the sackcloth and exhort all within voice shot. We are called to be His messenger: "Believe in the Lord Jesus Christ, the Son of God, Whose coming in glory is imminent and inevitable." For we are but moments from the saintly chorus which will resound throughout all creation:

"The kingdoms of this world are become the kingdoms of our Lord, and of his Christ; and he shall reign for ever and ever" (Revelation 11:15)

Notes

[1] When George H.W. Bush spoke before Congress, it was September 11, 2000, eleven years to the day before 9/11, a number itself which oozes with occult implications.

[2] From Jim Garrison, *America as Empire: Global Leader or Rogue Power? p. 193.*

[3] In 1984, George Orwell introduced us to several new terms like *doublethink* and *newspeak,* but has been inaccurately credited with *doublespeak . . .* but it is all just *doubletalk*! See http://www.orwelltoday.com/dblspkthennow.shtml.

[4] This program of the U.S. Treasure and Federal Reserve inflated our currency and therefore, reduced our debt in real money terms.

[5] It began in December, 2010.

[6] Such as spying on friendly foreign embassies and countless millions in the European Union, hacking into any computer system of any country in the world we choose to compromise.

[7] Including the family friendly Mormons like Mitt Romney and pious supporters too theologically naïve to tell the difference between biblical evangelicalism and the Mormon counterfeit.

[8] "Contrary to common belief, the phrase "entangling alliances" was turned by Thomas Jefferson, not George Washington. Washington advised against "permanent alliances," whereas Jefferson, in his inaugural address on 4 March 1801, declared his devotion to "peace, commerce, and honest friendship with all nations, entangling alliances with none." See http://www. answers.com/topic/entangling-alliances#ixzz2Y6TbB5qr.

[9] Ned Beatty played the head of the Network, while Peter Finch won an Oscar for his role as Howard Beal, the Television News anchor, who became "The Mad Prophet of the Airways."

[10] The saying of John Dalberg-Action, "Power tends to corrupt, and absolute power corrupts absolutely in such manner that great men are almost always bad men."

[11] Adolph Hitler, *A Chilling Tale of Propaganda*, Dr. Otto Dietrich, The Third Reich's Press Secretary, p. 20, Typhoon International, 1999.

[12] During his first Presidential Campaign, Obama drew 200,000 cheering Germans to the same spot and received accolades not heard there in 75 years. Who was that equally inspiring orator speaking there in the 1930s?

[13] Japanese Imperialism was instrumental, of course, in the Pacific Theater, joining Germany and Italy as the Asian counterpart of the Axis Powers.

[14] Francis A. Schaeffer, *Death in the City*, Downers Grove, Inter-Varsity Press, 1969, p. 209.

When Antichrist Reveals Himself in America, Will We Recognize Him?

By Douglas W. Krieger and S. Douglas Woodward

"So long as they concern themselves with their religious problems the State does not concern itself with them. But so soon as they attempt by any means whatsoever—by letters, Encyclical, or otherwise—to arrogate to themselves rights which belong to the State alone we shall force them back into their proper spiritual, pastoral activity."

Adolf Hitler in a speech delivered in Berlin on the May Day festival, 1937

This essay is drawn from *The Final Babylon: America and the Coming of Antichrist* and also published in *Blood on the Altar*, Tom Horn Author and Editor

IN THIS ESSAY, WE EXPLORE THE WORDS OF ADOLF HITLER AND HOW HIS SINCERE CONVICTION LED THE GERMAN NATION TO AFFIRM HIM TO BE THEIR SAVIOR. INSTEAD, HE BECAME THE ANTICHRIST OF THE TWENTIETH CENTURY. IS A SIMILAR SET OF CIRCUMSTANCES TRANSPIRING IN AMERICA TODAY? WILL THE EVANGELICAL CHURCH IN AMERICA BE COMPLICIT IN ANTICHRIST'S ASCENDANCY AS IT WAS IN NAZI GERMANY?

Political Professions of Faith

TO THE SURPRISE AND THE DISMAY OF MOST CHRISTIANS, IT IS PROBABLE NO REPELLENT POLITICAL FIGURE IN MODERN TIMES EVER PROFESSED FAITH IN CHRISTIANITY MORE THAN ADOLF Hitler. No public official ever championed the separation of Church and State more fervently than the Führer. And it is unlikely any religious leader promoted putting faith into action with more exuberance than the leader of the National Socialist Party. Consider a small sample of Hitler's words:

> "This 'Winter Help Work' [a social 'outreach' program] is also in the deepest sense a Christian work. When I see, as I so often do, poorly clad girls collecting with such infinite patience in order to care for those who are suffering from the cold while they themselves are shivering with cold, then I have the feeling that they are all apostles of a Christianity—and in truth of a Christianity which can say with greater right than any other: this is the Christianity of an honest confession, for behind it stand not words but deeds." [1]

Figure 9 - Luther's The Jews and their Lies

For these substantive reasons and many more (not always so warmly swaddled in biblical ideals), the German Catholic as well as 'Evangelical' Church *failed to discern a glaring and provocative manifestation of Antichrist in their midst*. The best and the brightest, the priests and the theologians, all were caught up in the rush to support the cause of National Socialism. German leaders, both spiritual and political, stood side-by-side to bring the Fatherland back from the brink. And Adolf Hitler inspired them to come together for the common cause.

Certainly, more than 'mass psychology' was influencing 1930s Germany. [2] Christian intellectuals, from the middle ranks to the upper echelons, professed faith in the Führer. In hindsight, we could be justifiably aghast how the experts wholly missed the most obvious incarnation of the Antichrist since brutal first-century Roman emperors fed thousands of Christians to the lions. [3] How, pray tell, could this happen?

Indeed, this particular "mystery of iniquity" (2 Thessalonians 2:7) astonishes us because Hitler not only convinced the hungry and unemployed masses — he gained the favor of the theologically sophisticated. Despite his outspoken rancor and the suspected occultism amongst him and his accomplices, opposition from the Church never materialized in any meaningful way until almost the War's end. Hitler promoted what Germans wanted to hear—*that God was on their side.* He provoked patriotism by calls to revere the old ways. He assured the nation that the disgrace of losing 'the Great War' (World War I) had nothing to do with the Kaiser's blatant imperialism. And despite outrageous anti-Semitism, Adolf Hitler was hailed as 'God's man of the hour.' The servants of God were simply clueless in detecting the malevolent motivating force behind Adolf Hitler. *Discernment disappeared from the Church.*

Behold the uniqueness of Adolf Hitler! With contagious conviction he voiced what the German soul could be in its manifold creative genius! His carefully orchestrated words disclosed complete commitment and utter brilliance as a leader of the people. With rapturous expressions, he invigorated a dejected Germany. He guided the rediscovery of its powerful but pagan roots, illuminating who they were and what they could become, with Almighty God guiding their steps (he saw no conflict between Odin and Jehovah!) Hitler injected into nearly every German heart a DIVINE IMPRIMATUR which justified an inferno of destruction and death unmatched in human history. Its pristine message created a new Reich of *DAS VOLK*, a people destined by the triumph of their collective will to become the consummation and commencement of the Kingdom of God—DAS

THOUSANDE JAHRE REICH (the millennial reign, a one-thousand-year kingdom initiated in the German spirit of Charlemagne, the emperor of the FIRST REICH, the *Holy Roman Empire* inaugurated at Christmas 800 AD). [4]

This infamous would-be Kaiser/Caesar/Antichrist arose in Germany over a ten-year timeframe, from the end of 1924 until he became Chancellor in March 1933, and soon thereafter, becoming the supreme leader—having combined the offices of President and Chancellor into 'Führer and Reichskanzler' upon the death of President Paul von Hindenburg.

There were those, however, who possessed the ability to discern the real meaning of National Socialism. They possessed the necessary time and skill to analyze the political, social, and spiritual events leading up to the Nazi takeover. But they steadfastly refused to respond to their better judgment. No doubt their failure in part stemmed from a latent (and all-too-often blatant) anti-Semitism wide-spread amongst the German population, arguably stimulated by Martin Luther's strong anti-Semitic perspectives. [5] Nevertheless, even the dramatic incidents of hate expressed toward Jews (one thinks of *Kristallnacht, Crystal Night* or *the Night of the Broken Glass,* November 9-10, 1938) failed to supply the spiritually astute with insight into what was going to happen. The appeal of Hitler satisfied a number of concerns related to national pride, providing simple

Figure 10 - God with Us

answers to very complex questions, promising economic rebirth to a nation dead in its fiscal tracks, and the rehashing of the nation's favorite Teutonic folk myths stirring the soul of its people.

We don't have space to concern ourselves with *all* the causes for the *apokalypsis* of Antichrist in Germany.[6] Instead, we will focus on the spiritually-based sentiments Hitler explicitly expressed, promising that his ideology and his government supported the Christian faith—that there was no conflict between National Social-ism and Christianity. It was this relationship—an overtly rank expression of 'religio-political apostasy'—which so disturbs us. From his countless statements made directly to Christian audiences, we will learn why Adolf Hitler was so extremely dangerous. Surprisingly (we think you will agree ours is not the standard interpretation), it was not because he could scheme so treacherously. To the contrary, the key to Hitler's sleight-of-hand was due to his own self-delusion: he possessed unwavering faith that his was a righteous calling from God above—wrought by 'providence.'

Figure 11 - Reichskirche Flag

Our point in this piece: Beware! Similar circumstances are present in our land today. Americans must be on guard—especially at this most portentous time—with depressed economic conditions, a high unemployment rate, and smooth talking politicians long on promises and short on accomplishments. Our vigilance cannot be dulled even by the most sincere sounding statements of faith and vision from prominent public figures. Our observations must be focused on not just what is said, but what is being done. A superficial assessment will not suffice. We must consider all the evidence carefully and draw conclusions in pious contemplation. The Church (both liberal and conservative) is poised to fail miserably in recognizing who the real enemy is.

Our concern boils down to this poignant question: *If Antichrist were to be revealed in America, would the faithful recognize him?*

Would Americans committed to spiritual values miss the same clues disclosing Antichrist's true nature as did the Germans with Hitler?

There is little doubt that if a figure paraded himself in front of the American people resembling an easily stereotyped leader of the Third Reich—with a mousy moustache, an armband with a hypnotic logo, and wearing a brown shirt—his character and agenda would be obvious to almost everyone. Mounting the podium with an emotional appeal to our national loyalty, the adamant display of venom and vitriol against the enemies of the State, the promise of the restoration of our American 'empire' through a continuing buildup of military might, the stark name-calling identifying an appropriate scapegoat to fault for our problems—all of these factors would, at best, betray a would-be antichrist figure as a false messiah—or at worst, spotlight an artless actor who undoubtedly took us for fools.

We can be certain the *apocalypse* of (that is, the *revealing* of) Antichrist in America, an event we believe will transpire in the years just ahead, will be a one-of-a-kind challenge requiring spiritual discernment worthy of only the most circumspect and attuned 'code breakers' whose specialty is exposing wolves in sheep's clothing. We call the Church to take up this mission. We believe the Church of Jesus Christ, the true Church that understands the authentic meaning of Jesus' message, the coming of The Kingdom of God, stands as the last line of defense.

Orchestrating the Madding Crowd

Remember Hitler achieved a meteoric rise to prominence and power because he understood the soul of his people. He could relate. He knew what made them tick. He realized how to couch his message in the context of the political situation and how to engage those who would be but mere spectators by relating to their financial pain and anxiety over the future. Hitler understood crowd psychology and how to manipulate it. To mesmerize his audience, he utilized the power of emphatic facial expressions and energetic hand gestures.

He compelled unquestioning allegiance by conveying solutions plainly and confidently no matter how oversimplified or extreme his answers might be. In fact, the more oversimplified and uncompromising his solutions were, the better to persuade the people of their usefulness. His greatest weapon was that "wretched Treaty of Versailles" and its national humiliation—its guilt-ridden condemnation upon the German people, coupled with horrific war reparations heaped upon the German people (which Capitalists in America were only too happy to finance).

What is the lesson for us? If the Antichrist were to arise in America at this moment, we would be foolish to expect him to be anything but a consummate American. He would look like us. He would talk like us. He would think—for the most part—like us. And with a straight face he might even assert a profession of Christian faith, and why he believes the teaching of Jesus Christ is so well suited for society. Following Adolf Hitler's lead, he would appeal to the most devout class of Christian, the Evangelical. He would offer opportunities to bring biblically-based believers 'out front'—to escape the shadows of social disdain and distance themselves from the hackneyed portrait showcased by the media and affirmed by the intelligentsia, supposing that those who call themselves Evangelical are intellectually bankrupt. He would convince Bible-believing conservatives that they should no longer see themselves as simple *plebeians* (common folk). Their self-image should be elevated so they regard their value no less in status than the progressive patricians of sophisticated national institutions.[7] Not that he would identify himself with the elite nor propose that the common man should be ashamed of his laborer status. Rather, he would argue he remains a man 'of the people' yet holds himself sufficiently apart to sanctify his status as our formidable if not *fearless* leader.

This *positioning* reflects the example of Herr Hitler in many respects. Likewise, the tone and substance coming from the mouth of the Führer, although etched in the *zeitgeist* of that age, begs for comparison to what we hear today from select political leaders promoting the American version of The New World Order[8], especially those who were, are, or would be our President. Consider for a moment: might it not be a factor in the false Christ's persuasiveness—the fact that he could "*deceive, if possible, even the elect*"? (Matthew 24:24).

The sham to fool Evangelicals will make use of more than patronizing remarks. It will turn the words of our most popular preachers against us. The ideology that should prohibit the arising of Antichrist—the Christian religion and its worldview—will be a powerful tool co-opted to capture the 'believing' masses and to encourage through a moral veneer and political resolution an agenda resonating within the heart of the 'folks' in these United States. Indeed, the future philosophy of Antichrist will convince us we should resolve to be nothing less than what *our most prominent spiritual leaders teach us to be—successful, healthy, and committed to classic American ideals* (although our most noble notions of individual liberty, *a la* Henry David Thoreau and Thomas Jefferson, have long since quietly departed for destinations unknown).

In like manner, Antichrist would deftly implore citizens to follow his lead. He would criticize Christians for their failure to follow the most 'positive' aspects of our faith. Indeed, it would be similar to Hitler's 'Positive Christianity'—a Christianity that is proactive, expressed in 'unselfish service' to others, characteristic of true Americans.

He would call us to be the best Americans we can be—a worthy aspiration for the greater good of all Americans. The health of our nation, he would argue, depends upon living productive lives that contribute to economic prosperity for all. Morality, like ethics, should be shaped to improve our communities in light of standards established by the majority. Religion, true religion, will instill these values. It will not conflict with political objectives because *positive* faith goes hand-in-hand with constructive political ideology. The manifesto of 'the public good' will brand any substantial opposition worthy of elimination. True believers will be activists—but for causes that conform to the will of the many—all the better to reflect his 'image,' with *"great signs and wonders to deceive"* (Matthew 24:24).

On the surface, the nature of these ideals will seem consistent with the Bible. After all, who would argue that the spiritually inclined should be unproductive, immoral, unethical, a burden on the public's well-being, and incapable of contributing to the community's economic health? And yet, upon a more cautious objective inspection, there will emerge a thin but distinctive line between a laudable social compact (built upon beneficial principles for both the individual and the nation) and an overreaching 'State' that demands unquestioned obedience (aka *cooperation*)—commanding allegiance above all other causes no matter how worthy. One thinks of the Pro-life stance denying women the right to choose. American Society has chosen Pro-abortion. There are over 50 million dead Americans that never made it outside the womb to gain some semblance of civil rights. Those who point out this sorry fact are liable to be labeled 'social dissidents.'

Figure 12 - The Cross and the Swastika

Moreover, the challenge to discern the agenda of the Antichrist will be difficult for many reasons, not just intellectual. Social pressure to conform will be 'maxed out.' The path to achieve clarity will be a lonely path, for our peers will be only too ready to encourage complicity. Any complaint and disparagement will be interpreted as unpatriotic, a threat to social order, and harmful not only to our own health, but to those we love and care about. An 'untoward behavior' will be viewed as 'self-alienation,' first frowned upon, and then doggedly condemned since it fails to benefit 'the many.' One's consciousness-raising must be done in stealth so as not to draw attention to an expressed awareness that the enemy of Christ speaks profanely in our presence. It will not be easy to resist even if we were to come to the realization we have been asked to serve Antichrist. *Our peers will plead with us not to rock the boat, not to question falling in line, not to label the State as anything but what is best for one and all.* To be 'the best Christian one can be' will appear synonymous with being the perfect U.S. citizen. Fear will lead families to betray one another: brother will betray brother, children will betray their parents, and all in the name of doing what is 'for the common good of all.' The words of Jesus from the Gospel of Matthew must be seen for what they really are: a sign of His soon coming.

21 And the brother shall deliver up the brother to death, and the father the child: and the children shall rise up against their parents, and cause them to be put to death.

22 And ye shall be hated of all men for my name's sake: but he that endureth to the end shall be saved. (Matthew 10:21, 22)

Needing to recognize political and religious rhetoric as a potential harbinger of the evil one to come, study the words of Hitler below. He seems most open-minded. Consider just how difficult it will be to discern the voice of Antichrist when it reverberates in America:

"We demand liberty for all religious denominations in the State, so far as they are not a danger to it and do not militate against the morality and moral sense of the German race. The Party, as such, stands for positive Christianity, but does not bind itself in the matter of creed to any particular confession." [9] [Emphasis added]

"The National Government regards the two Christian Confessions as the weightiest factors for the maintenance of our nationality. They will respect the agreements concluded between them and the federal States. Their rights are not to be infringed . . . It will be the Government's care to maintain honest co-operation between Church and State; the struggle against materialistic views and for a real national community is just as much in the interest of the German nation as in that of the welfare of our Christian faith. The Government of the Reich, who regard Christianity as the unshakable foundation of the morals and moral code of the nation, attach the greatest value to friendly relations with the Holy See and are endeavoring to develop them." [10]

The partnership of Church and State constructed by Hitler was remarkable in many ways for he appealed to Christians' proclivity to self-righteous aspiration, beguiling them through awarding accreditation as possessors of the very "moral soul" of the nation. To enhance his appeal, *he vowed that without a Christian moral foundation, there would be no German morality.* In light of this, the reader of the Gospels can stop wondering why Jesus (in Matthew Chapter 24) was so repetitious regarding 'deception and being deceived,' 'false prophets and false messiahs,' and the like in reference to the 'state of society' at the end of the age.

At the time, his audience was Catholic, but his announcement of the Concordat with Rome (the papal agreement, July 5, 1933) had meaning to Protestants as well. The message was obvious and clear: friendly relations—relations that are inclusive of the Church—must be the norm in a resurgent Germany. "The fact that the Vatican is concluding a treaty with the new Germany means the acknowledgement of the National Socialist state by the Catholic Church. This treaty shows the whole world clearly and unequivocally that the assertion that *National Socialism [Nazism] is hostile to religion is a lie*." [11]

Hitler was even more effusive about the value of Nazism to benefit the Church:

> While we destroyed the Center Party [a Catholic political party [12], we have not only brought thousands of priests back into the Church, but to millions of respectable people we have restored their faith in their religion and in their priests. The union of the Evangelical Church in a single Church for the whole Reich, the Concordat with the Catholic Church, these are but milestones on the road, which leads to

the establishment of a useful relation and a useful co-operation between the Reich and the two Confessions. [13]

The Division of Labor in the Third Reich

Furthermore, it was essential *to separate the realms of personal faith from political action.* Hitler's 'spheres of function' were altogether essential insofar as the Church's dominion was concerned, for without the spiritual health of Germany, there would be no political health. But he also took a hard line to distinguish their responsibilities: the Church was to look after the spiritual and moral health of the flock—the State would tend to its material need:

> "The German Church and the People are practically the same body. Therefore there could be no issue between Church and State. The Church, as such, has nothing to do with political affairs. On the other hand, the State has nothing to do with the faith or inner organization of the Church." [14]

> "The National Socialist State professes its allegiance to positive Christianity. It will be its honest endeavor to protect both the great Christian Confessions in their rights, to secure them from interference with their doctrines (Lehren), and in their duties to constitute a harmony with the views and the exigencies of the State of today." [15] [Emphasis added]

> "So long as they concern themselves with their religious problems the State does not concern itself with them. But so soon as they attempt by any means whatsoever—by letters, Encyclical, or otherwise—to arrogate to themselves rights which belong to the State alone we shall force them back into their proper spiritual, pastoral activity." [16]

In other words, both Church and State must reassure its denizens the institution exists to provide for their well-being. But it is, from Hitler's perspective, necessary they split duties. Keep the Church's message personal and positive while the State should keep on its message of economic welfare for all. And of course, the supremacy of the State must be upheld. It was never to be questioned. The State dictated the role of the Church. Furthermore, it mandated that any criticism of the State would not be tolerated.

Moreover, upon close inspection, Hitler would 'gerrymander' the territory of the State whenever it suited him. Some theological modifications would be necessary. In a Germany liberated from the 'old-fashioned' faith, the Church should dismiss any talk of humankind's sinful inclinations and its need for repentance. *Evil must be mitigated—more specifically, downgraded—and reduced in substance to 'mistakes' and not the more menacing notion of sin.* Defects in human behavior amount to little more than 'poor choices.' Thus, with sin redefined and evil eliminated as a 'metaphysical reality' [17] the Gospel was compromised and the Church complicit. It could then pray reverently with the Führer:

> We want honestly to earn the resurrection of our people through our industry, our perseverance, and our will. We ask not of the Almighty, 'Lord, make us free!'—we want to be active, to work, to agree together as brothers, to strive in rivalry with one another to bring about the hour when we can come before Him and when we may ask of Him: 'Lord, Thou seest that we have transformed ourselves, the German people is no longer the people of dishonor, of shame, of war within itself, of faintheartedness and little faith: no, Lord, the German people has become strong again in spirit, strong in will, strong in endurance, strong to bear all sacrifices.' 'Lord, we will not let Thee go: bless now our fight for our freedom; the fight we wage for our German people and Fatherland.' [18]

Furthermore, while the Führer did not directly confront Christian sensibilities, his prayer led one to conjecture as to what 'positive Christianity' involved, and exactly what its opposite—'negative Christianity'—would entail. No doubt his listeners let the matter drop without questioning the meaning behind his exhortation for accentuating a 'positive Christianity.' In contradistinction, like observing a lit firecracker failing to pop, we should be very alarmed when such a loaded phrase lies dormant for too long. The observer must be asleep if they have no apprehension about when the firecracker *will* detonate.

To the wary spectator, Hitler's statement anticipated a pause 'for the other shoe to drop.' And yet, assuming nothing but good intent from the Führer, the audience did not worry one iota that another shoe would hit the floor (or worse, the fecal matter would collide with the oscillating rotor!) Instead, they were enraptured by Hitler's acclamation:

> MY LORD AND SAVIOR . . . IN THE BOUNDLESS LOVE AS A CHRISTIAN . . . HE HAD TO SHED HIS BLOOD UPON THE CROSS. My feelings as a Christian point me to my Lord and Savior as a fighter. It points me to the man who once in loneliness, surrounded only by a few followers, recognized these Jews for what they were and summoned men to fight against them [Peter should take up his sword, rather than put it away]. This is God's truth! He was greatest not as a sufferer but as a fighter. In boundless love as a Christian and as a man I read through the passage which tells us how the Lord at last rose in His might and seized the scourge to drive out of the Temple the brood of vipers and adders. How terrific was His fight for the world against the Jewish poison. Today, after two thousand years, with deepest emotion I recognize more profoundly than ever before in the fact that it was for this that He had to shed His blood upon the Cross. As a Christian I have no duty to allow myself to be cheated, but I have the duty to be a fighter for truth and justice . . . [19] [Emphasis added]

The notion that the Messiah was himself NOT Jewish was a view propounded by Richard Wagner, the famous German composer whose operas were expressions of the nineteenth-century German *Zeitgeist* (the 'spirit of the age'). Unquestionably, Hitler's favorite composer, Wagner, stirred Hitler's soul to envision a revived, irrepressible, and vengeful Germany. During World War II, Wagner's legacy lived on as his music filled the putrefied air of Holocaust death camps. As a result, survivors would forever associate Wagner with Auschwitz. This was no disservice to Wagner—for he believed that Christ was Aryan, not Jewish. And like Friedrich Nietzsche, the '*Philosopher Emeritus*' of the German people (a good friend of Wagner until their falling out), he believed the German soul must not be dragged down by the 'slave mentality' of the Jew. Consequently, it logically followed that Jesus could never be considered a Jew. To the aspiring German mindset, the Jews were a millstone about their necks. The Hebrew religion bestowed nothing but restrictive laws and depressive guilt. It was time for Germany to cast aside the Jewish mentality and its stifling effect upon the soul of humankind, but especially their Aryan race!

As to Nietzsche, he famously asserted a philosophy known as *the will to power.* To the extent Jesus allowed himself to be crucified, *to that same extent Jesus was Himself the anti-Christ.* For Nietzsche, Jesus' commitment to die for the sin of the world was nothing but a *death wish* to be condemned and repudiated. For him, Jesus' willingness to lay down his life remains the source of so much nonsense contaminating the true purpose for religion. Instead, a 'true confession' encourages struggle! (*Mein Kampf* of course means, *My Struggle*) For Nietzsche, suffering saves no one. Moreover, this must be the stalwart creed of all true believers. The gospel of Wagner, Nietzsche, and especially Adolf Hitler held in common a disdain for the Jew.

The duty to be a fighter for truth, justice (and the German way) comprises, of course, the motto of *Superman*, the quintessential American superhero. Indeed, less feted translators often seek to convey the meaning of Nietzsche's *Übermensch* with the expression *Superman.* However oversimplified this one-word translation (especially vulgar to the sophisticated), nonetheless, it likewise urges those loyal to Old Glory—the red, white, and blue—to stand and be counted! America boasts the greatest military ever assembled. Any concept of redemptive suffering preached from the Bible by ignoble vicars of Christ surely misses the mark. Turning the other cheek (Matthew 5:39) cannot be what Christ actually meant. "Fight back! Don't get mad—get even!" Of course, the German people in the 1920s and 1930s were a frustrated, defeated people, wearing anger on their sleeves right below their swastikas.

Americans do not feel compelled to take such overt military action. Discretion is the better part of valor. We much prefer to keep our battles on the 'down low', equipping our intelligence services to act covertly (witness the current, 2013 conflict regarding NSA's [National Security Agency] mining of private phone and Internet data, spying on multiple foreign (friendly) governments, accessing and cataloguing private data of one hundred million Americans, as well as the intrusive behavior of the Treasury Department's Internal Revenue Service), requiring our special forces to operate in darkness, and necessitating U.S. sorties of the aeronautical kind be carried out in stealth mode. As the military is wont to say, 'We own the night.' Unlike the saints to whom Paul addressed his letters, one could argue (and Woodward has in his books, *Power Quest—Books One and Two*), that in the last one hundred years, the U.S. government has seldom sought to be mistaken for *children of the day.*

Hating in the Name of Christ and Country

The unity of the Church was important to Hitler. He could not consummate his grand plan without the support of the Church. He required his back-side be covered. Consequently, it was crucial that disputes in the Church be silenced, if for no other reason than to keep quarrels from bubbling over into matters of State and distracting the populace from the bellicose but sacred duty before them.

> It will at any rate be my supreme task to see to it that in the newly awakened NSDAP, the adherents of both Confessions can live peacefully together side by side in order that they may take their stand in the common fight against the power, which is the mortal foe of any *true* Christianity [as Hitler would define it]. [20]

> This is for us a ground for satisfaction, since we desire that the fight in the religious camps should come to an end... all political action in the parties will be forbidden to priests for all time, happy because we know what is wanted by millions who long *to see in the priest only the comforter of their souls and not the representative of their political convictions* [emphasis added]. [21]

Furthermore, Hitler required that the Church's energy contribute to the Fatherland's *fighting spirit*. Christ must not be seen as the Prince of Peace. Religious fires must burn brightly on his behalf.

> So far as the Evangelical Confessions are concerned we are deter-mined to put an end to existing divisions, which are concerned only with the forms of organization, and to create a single Evangelical Church for the whole Reich . . . And we know that were the great Ger-man reformer [Martin Luther] with us today he would rejoice to be freed from the necessity of his own time and, like Ulrich von Hutten [1488–1523, an outspoken German scholar, poet and reformer], his last prayer would be not for the Churches of the separate States: *it would be of Germany* that he would think . . . and of the Evangelical Church of Germany [Hitler loved putting words in the mouth of Mar-tin Luther]. [22]

After all, to Hitler, the real enemy was the 'International Jew.' Christianity must unite, Catholics and Protestants, laity and priest-hood—"against the power"—i.e., the international Jewish conspiracy that, he argued, warred against the Church of Jesus Christ and the German people. Not that this tactic was especially risky. His ap-proach was tried and true—unite around a well-defined mutual foe. Foment hatred against the scapegoat. Exaggerate images to make plain their villainess ways. Build the faithful into the 'hammer of God' – make it an instrument of *righteous indignation!*

Impulse for a New Christian Ecumenism?

In comparison, today's political leadership in America and Eu-rope has it somewhat easy; *it does not need to manufacture a fanat-ical enemy*. RADICAL Islam has served itself up as the despicable lunatic fringe fighting against Christendom and the State. The polit-ical leadership message must be made plain to the public: the radical Muslim is not at war not with the actions of the American govern-ment; they hate us because of our 'way of life.' Their enmity is per-sonally directed at Americans. It could not be due to protectionism of American corporations supervised by the political system and safeguarded by the military. It could not be because we have military bases in their land. Nor could it be because we have helped ourselves to their petroleum. The words of our politicians insist it is our sacred values of freedom and faith in the Bible of both Old and New Testaments. From the speeches of our governing leaders, their disdain for *Americana* [23] is the primary reason why Islam hates Americans. Islam views the Church's toleration of secular society as an abhorrent mixture of the *sacred and profane*—not so much an expression of political unity, but a compromised expression of religious weakness.

Subsequently, the more Islam frightens the free world, the more its enemies (secular and religious) understandably and justifiably unite. Other than twisting its ulterior motive (making it about the differences in religion as the root cause for animosity),[24] why do we need to create falsehoods about the opposition when of its own accord it provokes with carefully crafted words of hate, carries out cowardly acts of terror, and callously celebrates death when it completes its missions of murder? Radical Islam deserves disdain. Their terrorist acts are deplorable. Still, there are some legitimate reasons why they hate the United States.

Notwithstanding the subtleties in analyzing the causes for Islamic hatred of the USA, the pathway to co-opt the Church in America today first requires the encouragement of unity within the varied hallowed institutions, then secondly, aligning them according to the preferred political agenda. The broad strategy for managing religious institutions has not changed all that much over the past eighty years—although selected tactics do differ.

So what is the method to achieve an ecumenical union? It involves reconstructing the Christian message. Building unity in the contemporary church comprises a modern day equivalent to building the Tower of Babel. *The most relevant message, what will really bring us together as one, requires the church to substitute the content of the gospel with a message of confusion, which is what Babel means.* How can this be accomplished? By creating confusion over *the nature of good and evil.* We could say that reaching new heights in cooperation with other beliefs and faiths is not based upon clear communication and seeing things eye-to-eye. *It is about not seeing things at all.* 'Coming together' necessitates closing one's eyes to *see no evil, hear no evil,* and *speak no evil.* The less said the better. We must dispense with controversial matters, uniting against intolerance, epitomized in militant Islam. We can do no less. Indeed, regarding traditional Judeo-Christian values, the nature of sin and the reality of evil in particular, stand out like sore thumbs. Therefore, Church leadership in its aspiration seek to be mainstream Americans, must paper over the notion of sin and evil with platitudes of self-improvement, overcoming self-doubt, as well as proclaiming health and wealth to magically make their congregations (and especially them) wealthy. In today's Evangelical Church, it is most certainly about expressing a positive Christianity! Hitler would feel especially vindicated if he attended the typical Megachurch and listened to the sermons there. [25] Christianity has been effectively shorn of biblical discernment and blinded to the reality of evil as it presents itself in our world today.

Diminishing doctrine as an essential element in 'confessional Christianity' is hardly new. Liberal Christian Churches dispensed with meaningful theological content decades ago. They embraced a social gospel, replete with platitudes of pluralism, while promoting the practice of social good works, unwittingly leading to greater government intervention and involvement in the church. When American theologians sentenced God to death in the 1960s, they simultaneously (albeit unwittingly) assigned their own ecclesiastical institutions to death row. Fifty years ago, they reduced the Gospel to what was left over after so-called science ravaged the Bible. Theology became nothing more than existential philosophy. The meaning of being a Christian amounted to repeating holy words in ritual ceremonies. It did not matter how far out (i.e., how 'supernatural') the notions of the original creeds or 'Psalters' were. *Theology became applied psychology.* It was reconstructed to be a frame of mind or, better yet, a mental state. Once the Creeds had been ransacked of all calls to spiritual transformation and relieved of all genuine miracles recorded in the Bible, what remained was Schleiermacher's "feeling of absolute dependence," Tillich's ruminations about God as the "ground of being," or Karl Jasper's yearning for an "ultimate experience." Consequently, today's mainstream churches are now so emaciated it is a wonder they have not already given up the ghost.

In contrast, today's Evangelical churches (that proclaim that oh-so-positive message) swarm with 'believers'. But the question is, "What do they believe in?" To be sure, there are many assemblies of faithful, believing Christians that keep science in its place and rightly esteem spiritual reality; who regard the Bible as God's Word; and rely upon the Spirit of Christ to be an ever-present reality in their daily lives—not so much as an emotional impulse stimulating a mystical faith, but as an enabling power to conquer the challenging circumstances of everyday life. On the other hand, as we contend, the most well-known churches appear guilty of depriving their congregations of meaningful content—biblically-based content. It is almost as if the Gospel so successfully preached there today is derived from aphorisms in *Poor Richard's Almanac*: "Early to bed and early to rise makes a man healthy, wealthy, and wise." Or to misquote a famous mega-church preacher: "It IS about you!" Or worse yet, the Evangelical message transforms spirituality into a transaction: You do "x" and God does "y." "Give and it shall be given to you"—*not out of need but out of greed.* God *guarantees* our destiny to be healthy, wealthy, and wise (although the last item in this threesome is not always requested). At issue is only whether you count yourself entitled to merchandise from the Heavenly commissary, stocked wall-to-wall to assure your material needs are met in full.

Betraying the Meaning of the Kingdom of God

After the death of Pope Pius XI in 1939, the electoral procedure to seat another Pope began. The election favored Eugenio Pacelli (1876–1958) and four days later, Pacelli made it clear that he would handle all German affairs personally. He proposed the following to Hitler:

> To the Illustrious Herr Adolf Hitler, Fuhrer and Chancellor of the German Reich! Here at the beginning of our Pontificate, we wish to assure you that we remain devoted to the spiritual welfare of the German people entrusted to your leadership. . . . During the many years we spent in Germany, We did all in our power to establish harmonious relations between Church and State. Now that the responsibilities of our pastoral function have increased our opportunities, how much more ardently do we pray to reach that goal. May the prosperity of the German people and their progress in every domain come, with God's help, to fruition!

Pacelli was crowned Pope on March 12, 1939 (becoming Pius XII). The following month on April 20, 1939, at Pius XII's expressed wish, Archbishop Orsenigo, the nuncio (ambassador) in Berlin,

Figure 13 - The Pope's Nuncio, Archbishop Orsenigo

opened a gala reception for Hitler's fiftieth birthday. The birthday greetings thus initiated by Pacelli immediately became a tradition:

each April 20 during the few years left to Hitler and his Reich, Cardinal Bertram of Berlin would send "warmest congratulations to the Fuhrer in the name of the bishops and the dioceses in Germany," to which he added "fervent prayers which the Catholics in Germany are sending to heaven on their altars." [26] *The walls of the Kingdom of God were thoroughly breached. The homogenization of Church and State was complete.*

In the context of today's Megachurch, we must ask, "What does the Kingdom of God mean?" It is a most unwelcomed question since many of our ministers and theologians in America do not proclaim a 'coming Kingdom'—such a prophetic assertion implies a negative message. If the Kingdom exists at all, many churches preach it is up to us to 'take dominion' and bring it about ourselves. Like Hitler, we 'struggle' (the meaning behind *mein kampf*) to make it real. How odd, then, that we who foresee the Kingdom to be before us (in the future) to proclaim America could truly be that 'City on a Hill' beckoning the 'huddled masses' (yearning to be free) to come be a part of our melting pot.

This phrase, 'The Kingdom of God', was the theme of Jesus' ministry. It was his 'call to action'—his byword, his catchphrase. Despite that being so, given what appears to be the *modus operandi* of megachurches, we question whether the coming of the Kingdom of God resides at the center of today's preaching. No, the preaching of our most celebrated churches resounds with a different message.

We believe its common creed is rather crass. It is at least as materialistic as it is spiritual. It is about getting the most out of life—or better yet, making the most (money) you can! In fact, one's financial independence indicates your spiritual status. The manner of making your life count is measured in denominations of $20s, $50s, and $100s. Jesus' blunt injunction about deciding between two masters, God and mammon (material prosperity), seems intentionally withdrawn. *God wants you to have all the mammon you can muster*! If the Apostles showed up in a Megachurch today, chances are they would wonder what the message being proclaimed has to do with the faith for which they died. Jesus told his audience (much to their astonishment) that it is virtually impossible for the rich to enter into the Kingdom of God. It is easier for a camel to pass through the eye of a needle (Matthew 19:24). The real truth could not have been more out of step with their colloquial tradition. In their day, it was just common sense: prosperity meant God's affirmation—if you were rich, you were 'in like Flynn.' You were as valuable in the Kingdom of God as your net worth—and not a penny less. That is why Jesus' message crashed his disciples' worldview like a brick landing on a paper airplane. Or better yet, a margin call on an over-leveraged portfolio.

Is it any wonder that the topic of prophecy is so taboo in most megachurches today? The true biblical apocalyptic message of Jesus Christ guarantees that private property means next to nothing—the world is passing away! Riches are of no value. Wealth will be consumed in the fire of the last days! *"I have come to cast fire upon the earth; and how I wish it were already kindled!"* (Luke 12:49)

To be sure, Jesus taught many parables based on the priority of keeping one's eyes peeled—the parables of readiness (Matthew 24:32-51 and Matthew 25) resoundingly affirm such a prescient posture: the "wise and foolish virgins"; the "sheep and the goats"; the traveling "master of the vineyard" (to name but a few). Nevertheless, His point was consistent (paraphrasing, but only slightly): *"Watch! For you know not when the Son of Man cometh."* (Matthew 25:13) All too often, those weary of prophetic teaching cite those they deem obsessed with its message for failure to remember what Jesus said, *"For you do not know the day or hour of my return . . . wherein the son of man cometh"* as if His words were a concession to the impossibility of living life in light of His charge—or as if His intent was granting license to ignore the *temporal* implication in the apocalyptic message, since we cannot tell when it will happen. But that is most assuredly the opposite of what Jesus taught. His words could not have been more plain—or provocative. "The world is ending! Be ready. Do not focus on wealth. Do not sequester treasure for yourself! Do not build bigger barns! Live one day at a time."

Indeed, the strategic plan for Kingdom members amounts to re-membering 'You can't take it with you'—so better to share the wealth with your brothers and sisters (not waste it on your every whim!). To quote our Lord in His own words:

> ¹⁹ *Lay not up for yourselves treasures upon earth, where moth and rust doth corrupt, and where thieves break through and steal:*

> ²⁰ *But lay up for yourselves treasures in heaven, where neither moth nor rust doth corrupt, and where thieves do not break through nor steal:*

> ²¹ *For where your treasure is, there will your heart be also.* (Matthew 6:19-21)

A main point of prophecy and why it is indispensable to the Gospel: to keep life and material things in proper perspective.

Justification by the Providence of God

In 1939, Adolf Hitler summarized why he was so confident the Third Reich was imminent: "The National Socialist Movement has wrought this miracle. If Almighty God granted success to this work, then the Party was His instrument." [27] In retrospect the reader would be hard pressed to find a historical leader who levered faith, however skewed, more effectively as a power tool for REALPOLITIK. Hitler was almost unparalleled in the annals of leadership as a cham-pion for the relevance of spiritual belief. He saw man created by God, rewarded for his reliance upon God, and sustained when cooperating with Him on a grand scale. In Hitler, we confront a leader who aban-doned all self-consciousness—he was so tightly coupled with his con-stituency that they became of one mind. Yes, he learned the craft of public speaking like few others—maybe better than anyone. But we are dangerously mistaken if we regard his fervor *as only an act*. NO, he believed in what he was doing. He lost himself in his cause.

He was not tepid in faith, darting hither and thither, equivocating whenever the opportunity afforded itself. To the contrary, the leader of the Third Reich was a champion of conviction which was so 'in your face' it was contagious. If faith wavered, Hitler reinstated it, bolstering public confidence in his program for a new Germany. His power hinged on claiming that a brilliant destiny lay at Germany's feet. God's providence guaranteed success. In every darkened pathway, he claimed God would enlighten the path, and keep National Socialism on track because it fulfilled the Almighty's Plan. Hitler pleaded it, believed in it, and 'owned' what he stridently confessed. All doubt concerning Germany's mission fled from his presence because, as far as he was concerned, God mandated that the German people be ultimately victorious. History would demonstrate divine preference. God would honor Hitler's unfeigned devotion to his people. Listen to his confident faith:

> In this hour I would ask of the Lord God only this: that, as in the past, so in the years to come He would give His blessing to our work and our action, to our judgment and our resolution, that He will safeguard us from all false pride and from all cowardly servility, that He may grant us to find the straight path which His Providence has ordained for the German people, and that He may ever give us the courage to do the right, never to falter, never to yield before any violence, before any danger... I am convinced that men who are created by God should live in accordance with the will of the Almighty... If Providence had not guided us I could often never have found these dizzy paths... Thus it is that we National Socialists, too, have in the depths of our hearts our faith. We cannot do otherwise; no man can fashion world history or the history of peoples unless upon his purpose and his powers there rests the blessings of this Providence. [28]

In the final analysis, the Antichrist may be dangerous not because he is the best actor ever to mount the world stage or that he will hide insincere intent and cloak satanic motive. He will be exceptionally treacherous because, like Adolf Hitler, he will be utterly convinced that defeat is inconceivable. *Convinced of his invincibility and even more, his infallibility, the deception characterizing the man of law-lessness will be utterly commanding because he is himself deceived, believing that God is evil and Satan good.*

> Only so you can appeal to your God and pray Him to support and bless your courage, your work, your perseverance, your strength, your resolution, and with all these your claim on life. [29]

> In this world him who does not abandon himself the Almighty will not desert. Him who helps himself will the Almighty always also help; He will show him the way by which he can gain his rights, his freedom, and therefore his future. [30]

Such sentiments cannot be dismissed because they are disingenuous. It would be preposterous to suppose Adolf Hitler was consistently inauthentic. He believed in an 'active cooperation' with the divine—his was a form of perseverance strengthened by a Calvinist-like conviction. Echoing the adage of the common man in America—*God helps those who help themselves!* Can we imagine a more *positive* way to express Christian faith? This maxim has almost been synonymous with home-grown American religion.

Perhaps it is to our advantage to listen to the words of Adolf Hitler and believe we must struggle and fight against our enemies. Perhaps we should put ourselves first. *Perhaps we should prioritize worldly riches, personal health, and not the Kingdom of God.*

Maybe we would be wise to forget the self-effacing teaching of the Master: *"He that findeth his life shall lose it: and he that loseth his life for my sake shall find it."* (Matthew 10:39) If so, it would also follow we should ignore the testimony of the aging Apostle Paul who was tormented by all manner of physical and emotional distress: *"Therefore I take pleasure in infirmities, in reproaches, in necessities, in persecutions, in distresses for Christ's sake: for when I am weak, then am I strong."* (2 Corinthians 12:10) Or maybe, to follow the logic of the Gospel of the Megachurch, Paul was just depressed in his old age!

No. If we believed what Paul believed, we would be willing to stand opposed to the State, be willing to sacrifice ourselves in the cause of the old-fashioned faith *"once delivered unto the saints"* (Jude 3), and find affliction, famine, peril, and suffering a way to draw close to God and be remade anew from the inside out. Surely that is a confession differing in kind and color. Of this one thing we can rest assured: the Führer would not approve. Dietrich Bonhoeffer talked about this plainly in his call to consecration in *The Cost of Discipleship*. Communion with Christ is manifest best when we participate and share in Christ's sufferings. We draw closest to Him, and He to us, not in our morning Bible Reading, not in our most emotional singing of choruses, but in suffering for the cause of Christ. Paul surely must be thinking of this reality when he said to the Church at Rome: *"And if children, then heirs; heirs of God, and joint-heirs with Christ; if so be that we suffer with him, that we may be also glorified together."* (Romans 8:17)

In closing, may we offer this call to discernment: beware the false flag operation, the burning of the 'Reichstag,' the diminution or even elimination of the People's Assembly (our Congress), and especially the coming of the Imperial leader in the name of heightened security and peace. For we have surely seen this before. Consequently, we are compelled to ask, "Are we awake? Are we vigilant at this moment in time when the stakes have never been higher? Are we prepared to be REAL CHRISTIANS when it means calling our government to question? Do we realize that most Christians will be against us when we challenge the actions of The State? Are we willing to follow the example of Bonhoeffer and stand opposed to the Antichrist even when he appears as the savior of the State and our way of life?"

"Those who cannot remember the past are condemned to repeat it." (Santayana)

Notes

[1] Adolf Hitler, speaking of the Winter Help Campaign on 5 Oct. 1937.

[2] "The main idea of Sigmund Freud's crowd behavior theory is that people who are in a crowd act differently towards people from those who are thinking individually. The minds of the group would merge to form a way of thinking. Each member's enthusiasm would be increased as a result, and one becomes less aware of the true nature of one's action." See http://cn.wikipedia.org / wiki/ Crowd_psychology.

[3] The study of who understood Hitler and fled and who did not is an intriguing study in itself. Walter Stein, student of Rudolph Steiner whom Trevor Ravenscroft credits with the story behind *The Spear of Destiny* fled to England. Paul Tillich who later became a major voice in American Theological Liberalism supposedly looked into the eyes of Hitler and saw the demonic and left for Switzerland. Dietrich Bonhoeffer stands out as the most noteworthy theologian who saw Hitler for what he was—a mass murderer. Eventually he lost his life for participating in an assassination attempt on Hitler. He constitutes the most famous Christian martyr of the twentieth century, although only one of millions as we have learned that the martyr death toll in the last twenty years may now exceed the total number of martyrs since the first century.

[4] Recall his true name was German, Karl the Great, in the line of Pepin, representing the dynasty of the Carolingians.

[5] Luther's *The Jews and Their Lies* (1543, Von den Jüden und iren Lügen) stands as the seminal statement on anti-Semitism. According to friend and scholar Gary Stearman, Luther makes his hatred for the Jews crudely plain.

[6] The Greek word, *apokalypsis*, means the revealing, particularly the revealing of deep secrets, from whence the word *apocalypse* derives.

[7] We might even have one of our most noteworthy evangelical leaders be asked to give the prayer at a Presidential Inauguration!

[8] Hitler spoke of bringing about the New World Order as did Franklin D. Roosevelt. George H.W. Bush made it his catch phrase.

[9] Item #24 of the German Worker's Party "Program" circa 1920s.

[10] Adolf Hitler, in his speech to the Reichstag on 23 March 1933

[11] Adolf Hitler, 22 July 1933, writing to the Nazi Party (quoted from John Cornwell's *Hitler's Pope.*)

[12] "The **German Centre Party** (German: *Deutsche Zentrumspartei* or just **Zentrum**) was a Catholic political party in Germany during the *Kaiserreich* and the Weimar Republic. In English it is often called the Catholic Centre Party. Formed in 1870, it battled the *Kulturkampf* which the Prussian government launched to reduce the power of the Catholic Church. It soon won a quarter of the seats in the Reichstag (Imperial Parliament), and its middle position on most issues allowed it to play a decisive role in the formation of majorities. "When the Nazis came to power the party dissolved itself on 5 July 1933 as a condition of the conclusion of a Concordat between the Holy See and Germany." See en.wikipedia.org/ wiki/Centre_ Party_ (Germany).

[13] Adolf Hitler, in his New Year Message on 1 Jan. 1934

[14] Adolf Hitler, answering C. F. Macfarland about Church & State (in his book, *The New Church and the New Germany*).

[15] Adolf Hitler, on 26 June 1934, to Catholic bishops to assure them that he would take action against the new pagan propaganda.

[16] Adolf Hitler, in a speech delivered in Berlin on the May Day festival, 1937

[17] By this we mean a reality in its own right, although C.S. Lewis was likely correct by describing *evil* not as essential to reality as "good" is, but akin more to "spoiled goodness"—lest we inadvertently fall into the conundrum of a Zoroastrian dualism where good and evil are on equal footing, or a Manichaeism in which God has two irreconcilable faces.

[18] Adolf Hitler, giving prayer in a speech on May Day, 1933

[19] Adolf Hitler from his speech of 12 April, 1922.

[20] Adolf Hitler, in the article "A New Beginning," 26 Feb. 1925

[21] Adolf Hitler, in a speech to the men of the SA at Dortmund, 9 July 1933, on the day after the signing of the Concordat (Agreement with the Roman Catholic Church, the Papacy).

[22] Adolf Hitler, in his Proclamation at the *Parteitag* at Nuremberg on 5 Sept. 1934.

[23] The Microsoft Dictionary supplies this definition. "All things peculiar to the United States' culture and people, anything that is a symbol of American life."

[24] Not that we believe Islam is "the religion of peace" as many of its followers maintain. Allah appears merciful only to his devout followers. Those who reject Islam deserve to lose their heads, at least according to the interpretation of the Koran from a large segment of the Muslim faithful. Tolerance is not a strong suit of Mohammed's teaching. If you doubt it, just publicly express the fact that Islam is intolerant and see how much intolerance it summons from Islamic followers.

[25] Indeed, Evangelical spiritual sentiment may be content to connect with nothing more than the name "Jesus." Without specific assertions, we possess nothing distinct or definite. Thus, the name of Jesus may stand for nothing. It is the ultimate use of the Lord's name in vain. There are those in leadership within the Church that would prefer to pray only to Jesus and talk about nothing but Jesus to avoid any sectarian debate. After all: *dogma divides; love abides.* Of course, that adage presumes *intuition* replaces *reason* as the sole religious faculty or means to discover reality. As Francis Schaeffer once conveyed, Evangelicals have their own form of religious mysticism that is just as elusive and ineffable as Buddist *koans*. In the final analysis, only *true truth* prevails (an awkward Schaefferian tautology meant to convey truth that is objective and universal—i.e., the opposite of relative "truth" or truth that is "caught" not "taught"). "Doctrineless sound bites" bite us all in the end.

[26] Cornwell, John, *Hitler's Pope: The Secret History of Pius XII*, Viking, 1999, p. 209.

[27] Adolf Hitler, in his proclamation to the German People on 1 Jan 1939.

[28] Adolf Hitler, in a speech at Wurzburg on 27 June 1937.

[29] Adolf Hitler, in a speech at Frankfurt on 16 March 1936.

[30] Adolf Hitler, in a speech at Hamburg on 20 March 1936.

Ancient Aliens and the Transformation of Humanity into Gods

By S. Douglas Woodward

"There is another narrative growing in public consciousness that can no longer be written off as mere fable: the idea that aliens from outer space or another dimension may have—or may be trying to—take control of the world."

Jim Marrs, from *Our Occulted History*

This essay was drawn from *Lying Wonders of the Red Planet: Exposing the Lie of Ancient Aliens*

> HERE I DISCUSS THE GROWING BELIEF THAT GOD IS NOT A SUPERNATURAL BEING, BUT MERELY AN ICON FOR ANCIENT ALIENS WHO NURTURED HUMANITY. FOR SOME, THIS SEEMS PREPOSTEROUS. FOR OTHERS, IT IS SELF-EVIDENT. IS ET DISCLOSURE COMING? IS THIS THE GREAT DECEPTION OF THE LAST DAYS? IS THE CHURCH AWARE AND WILLING TO FACE THIS UNFORESEEN THREAT?

The Paucity of Hope in America

AS THE TWENTIETH CENTURY CAME TO A CLOSE, AMERICA WAS FLEXING ITS FISCAL MUSCLES. FOR THE PRIVATE SECTOR, TIMES WERE GOOD. ECONOMICALLY, AMERICA ENJOYED BUDGET surpluses and low levels of unemployment. Wall Street was soaring. America's corporations were hitting on all cylinders.

On the other hand, the Public Sector could have been better. Hillary and Bill left the White House downcast after the Monica Lewinsky affair, making uncertain the lasting legacy of President Clinton. America inaugurated a new Republican President (Bush the Younger) only after it had been determined he had a few less 'hanging chads' than Democrat Al Gore. The lack of a decisive vote in the 2000 election created a constitutional crisis that a Supreme Court decision and a gracious Al Gore finally settled.

Likewise, the prognosis of America's spiritual health was not particularly encouraging. Mainline churches were losing members left and right while altruistic faith-based institutions (George H.W. Bush's 'thousand points of light') sputtered along too, often hampered by scandal. By any stretch, faith in the society's institutions was hardly hitting the high water mark.

Bucking the trend, however, were numerous non-traditional evangelical 'mega-churches.' Buttressed by their 'gospel of prosperity' (a good believer is a *wealthy* believer), promoting a positive message (bad things happen because of *bad attitudes*—so be upbeat!), and recasting the gospel so it would be 'seeker friendly' (preaching *agin'* sinning hurts attendance after all), many Americans' notion of God grew more loving as their view of evil's reality dissipated. A 'neo-evangelical' faith was born.

Cynical talk-show hosts and opinionated media moguls combined efforts to reset values about right and wrong, passed judgment on good and bad religion, and challenged the old-fashioned view of God (who reserved the right to punish the guilty and hold all humanity accountable to His rules). Since the horrific terrorist strikes were quickly judged an aberration of fanatical monotheists (not a symptom of humanity's fallen state), the spiritually inclined sought a more placid and accommodating sense of divine presence. No, the God of Abraham, Isaac, Jacob, (and even Jesus) should be purged of any vestiges of extreme ideological predispositions or unappealing, apparently dour, and surely ungracious behavior. Religious belief should spur us to good deeds, not fear or guilt. Never mind that this was an age old heresy Christianity weathered in the second and third centuries. [1] Americans, especially 'new-agers' and mega-church evangelicals had found this moralistic, vindictive God of the Old Testament most lacking in our day too. The transcendent 'god without' was replaced with the less accusatory and usually mollifying 'god within.' The wisdom of neo-evangelicals and secular humanists was converging.

Of course, who in their right mind (except those obscurantist fundamentalists) would argue otherwise? At least not in public. Clearly, our progressive culture and its need for an alternative god-concept mandated this comprehensive deity makeover.

In 2008, an enchanting new President emerged who had the audacity to hope government would solve societal problems. His enthusiasm enlivened politics as a potential savior and caused many to hope that this well-spoken and handsome young lad would revitalize America. With his spirited leadership, he would help us forget the inarticulate George 'W,' bank failures, economic crisis, quashed retirement funds, high unemployment, and the downside of runaway debt caused by quantitative easing. Wall Street was fingered as Public Enemy #1, deserving stiff penalties and demanding stronger regulations. If it couldn't be fixed, perhaps it should be 'occupied' until it was shut down. Health care for everyone would surely make things right in our nation. Visions of government grandeur twinkled in the eyes of socially-minded up-and-comers convinced that publically funded programs would fix what ailed us.

Alas, six years later, this optimism has been all but dashed. As we moved into 2014, the capacity of politics to make things better and the charming ways of our president had both proven unworthy as a certain place to pin our hopes. Like all other Federal regimes, this one has hardly proven immune to scandals, decisions made behind closed doors, and attacks on its enemies with unlawful abuse of power. Despite derision and threatened action targeting the excesses of investment banks, no one went to jail, demonstrating who really held all the cards. In the summer of 2013, an unfortunate series of events for the Administration snow-balled. The mainline media broke the IRS scandals to the public, the Edward Snowden affair disclosed we were spying on our allies, and proof became un-deniable that Big Brother *really was watching*. Indeed, given the revelations of the National Security Agency's (NSA) 'blanket eaves-dropping' on our cell phones and web queries, many concluded this edition of the Federal Government sought to restrict personal lib-erties even more than its Republican predecessor.

Who could have predicted that? And yet, never has the emer-gence of the police state seemed more probable than it does now. Critics had labeled the Administration *socialist*. But recent disclo-sures suggest it should be more accurately termed 'national socialist.' Whether true or not, the ranks of the disheartened and disillu-sioned swelled during 2013. Yes, the audacity of hope was too bold to come true. So now where should we place our hope?

On Our Own

Given this state of events, it seems reasonable to ask, reluctantly I might add, "Does America stand at the same crossroads as Europe did one hundred years ago?" Then, a battle weary and downtrod-den Europe looked for new leadership, no longer trusting in mon-archies. Instead, it elected a new regime who heeded the German philosopher king from four decades earlier, Friedrich Nietzsche, an iconoclastic author who boasted that 'God is dead' and man must make his own way. Old mores and values must be discarded. Hu-manity must choose its own principles by which to guide its individ-ual and social behaviors. God is irrelevant—only humanity answers the roll call. What Nietzsche meant by his notion of the *Übermensch* was precisely this: mankind stands alone. Therefore, we must shoulder all responsibility. *We shall overcome*—but without the help of God as represented by Jesus Christ. The lesson for us lest we forget: this was the functional philosophy of religion professed by Adolf Hitler—his perspective manifested the spirit of Antichrist in its ugliest incarnation.

Has America adopted the same *weltanschauung* as Germany did in 1923? It is understandable why we might conjecture the only way to carve a path through the jungle—to chart a new course—amounts to bald self-reliance. And if our 'selves' are not up to the task, maybe it is time we improve upon our circumstances with the knowledge of how to make our race stronger, better, and more resilient to the existential limitations we face. Maybe the only answer for human nature is to transcend our nature altogether. This was part of the plan of the Third Reich. Science and technology stood apart as THE source of hope. The pending promise of transhumanism, to alter our DNA that is, might just be the best and only real answer to our dilemmas. We do not know what the future holds—*but only we hold the future.* Thus Spoke Zoroaster, "God is dead." The Übermensch has come. Long live the Übermensch.

From this authors' perspective, should we come to that same conclusion in America (and we are on the verge of doing so), we best beware for we have forsaken the Bible's teaching regarding our sacred identity as image bearers of God. We forsake our birthright. By concluding we were NOT created in God's image, we choose to be transformed into the image of God's enemy. In a biblical cosmology, these are the only two choices. If we reject that cosmology, that worldview, that *weltanschauung,* we proclaim there exists no ontological necessity for good and evil. [2] That is, we deny good and evil are *realities* in our universe. And therein lies the greatest peril: *any society that denies evil is ready enthrone it.*

Nietzsche's call for humanity to remake God into man's image, to dismiss the notion of real good and evil, may appeal to the intellectual who overrates his or her place in the world, but it lacks appeal for the common man. Despite the skeptic's enduring challenge to question God's existence, humanity cannot quench its innate thirst for its maker: humankind will not accept the finality of an atheistic, materialist (i.e, *naturalist*) answer. There has to be a reason why we are here—there has to be someone out there who cares what happens to us. There must be someone mightier than we who made us what we are. Even if humanity ardently argues it has outgrown the need for God, it never stops looking for someone bigger than itself to explain why it exists. Such a quest comprises one of its most primal and persistent urges. We may alter our DNA, but the lesson learned from the Frankenstein monster still holds true: we will strive for our maker's affirmation.

While there are many in the 'Emergent Church' that adhere to the notion that our divinity lies within and through mysticism we may contact 'god' directly, many others remain unconvinced that our solution is spiritual in nature—especially if the proposed solution remains glued to an outmoded 'God' concept. They stand outside the newly revamped evangelical church looking for a solution from an *extraterrestrial* source, as odd as that may sound to the rest of us. This large and expanding group (which includes a sizeable swath of humanists and a burgeoning bevy of scientists who eschew total atheism) does not believe in any sort of a traditional god concept whatsoever. From whence shall their help come? The transcendent power sought lies beyond the terrestrial plane requiring leaps and bounds to the stars high above our heads.

Indeed, while some still persevere in our belief that God exists, an increasing segment of humanity has now been conditioned to dramatically alter its creed regarding the identity of deity and how we relate to him (or, as it were, 'THEM'). This affirmation—that our Creator and Nurturer *comes* from the stars rather than being *the One who made them*—constitutes the growing and perhaps most threatening *Great Deception* of the time in which we live, a time this author believes constitutes 'the last of the last days' before Jesus Christ returns to this earth. In fact, it appears to be a key part the final world religion predicted for two millennia. Like unbridled spiritualism, the belief in ET as our God, constitutes the ultimate religion of Mystery Babylon. If it is given sanction by the Roman

Catholic Church, which appears to be happening now, there remains little doubt it comprises exactly that. [3]

A New Spin on Religious Programming

Therefore, despite being a bit disheveled, belief in spiritual realities remains alive and well. The casual observer might not recognize the nature of spiritual yearning in today's world since it appears disguised in all manner of technology-enhanced video, high-definition multi-media graphics, and über-visual production values. Nonetheless, if we delve into the meaning of the mushrooming social phenomena associated with the highly strange and paranormal, we uncover that humanity still seeks the divine—albeit in odd places. To be specific, affirmations of faith show vivid signs of life in unexpected quarters. We see these creeds embedded in a few, formerly odd, but now successful television shows which captivate the masses. If the Lord tarries, these fringe notions will increasingly become main stream and will pose a most surprising and especially sinister threat to biblical Christianity and to the preservation of the image of God in humankind. Indeed, the threat exists already.

In this respect, no drama spellbinds us more than the TV quasi-documentary, *Ancient Aliens*. It provides a glimpse into the strange and no longer future worldview that beckons the up and comers—the Millennials. Produced by Prometheus Entertainment, *Ancient Aliens* has contributed mightily to the success of Cable TV's History Channel. From its website we read:

> Established in 1999, Prometheus Entertainment has been a leader in supplying critically acclaimed, highly-rated programming to the cable marketplace. The company has produced nearly 500 hours of dynamic and diverse television for clients such as History, A&E, E!, WEtv, Travel Channel, Bravo, Animal Planet, Lucasfilm Ltd., National Geographic Channel, AMC, Warner Bros–and more.

Just how successful has *Ancient Aliens* been? Quite successful. It just completed its fifth season and its producers have created a spinoff series. Debuting in 2014, *In Search of Aliens* will feature the usual crew of *Ancient Aliens* with Giorgio A. Tsoukalos (that guy with the crazy hairdo—formerly publisher of the now defunct *Legendary Times Magazine*), and Erich von Däniken—the infamous although mildly charming author of the cultural phenomenon, *Chariots of the Gods?* (1968). Due to its popularity, *Ancient Aliens* and Prometheus Entertainment are arguably the primary reasons the History Channel created a second cable channel, called simply 'H2'. *Ancient Aliens* was moved to H2 a couple of years ago (and *In Search of Aliens* will follow it there), no doubt to form the nucleus of its programming strategy as well as guarantee high ratings to attract advertisers.

So it is that sensational television has a new golden child. Cosmic wonders, UFOs, and the mysteries of ancient civilizations combine to advance extraordinary extraterrestrial credos. Not only does it make for great television, the programming provides fascinating answers to ultimate questions.

Thanks to *The History Channel* and Prometheus Entertainment, spiritual themes have been reintroduced to the public, pandering to our covert quest to understand where we come from. These techno-affirmations of faith ring true to many, thanks to both state-of-the-art media magic and a thorough baptism of pseudoscience. Who says we don't like to watch religious programming on television? My generation grew up watching *Davy and Goliath*. My kids grew up watching Star Wars and learning about *the Force*. Today, the out of this world all-wise spaceman has become the fashioner of this world.

As if their affront to traditional faith was not flagrant already, these same producers just recently (late 2013) brought forth *Bible Secrets Revealed*, an intentionally misnamed and ultra-misleading assault on orthodox perspectives of Bible truth. Based upon its name alone (*Prometheus* was the mythic Greek god who, with Aphrodite, fashioned humankind from the clay), we should have known where its producers were taking us.

Transforming Humanity into Gods

What would become of humanity if we believed our distant ancestors were not 'Earthlings' but Martians—if suddenly we were told that once we were 'star children' who came to Earth to realize a new and greater potential—to conquer a different world, a blue one as its surface was over 75% covered with water? What would we think if in the days ahead, visitors from another world appeared and demonstrated we shared a common genetic heritage? What if these humanoids—we will call them *Homo universalis* for want of a better name—showed how accepting a small bit of their DNA would solve our most difficult physiological and social issues? Might our government, even our religious leaders, entreat us to join the party with promises of greater health once we alter our physical attributes, our DNA, with the supposed advanced genetic material of the OTHERS? Why, they come in the name of evolution—to elevate us to the next phase of humanity! What if our leaders *demanded our compliance* for the good of society, to stamp out the inferior genetics of the 'old' human race?

Of course, this vision comprises only one scenario of what could be in the offing for humanity in these last days. It stands out, however, as a possibility we should contemplate, even guard against to the extent that that is possible, since so many well-regarded eschatological writer/researchers propose it to be the most likely manner in which the 'Mark of the Beast' (Revelation 13) will be made manifest. [4] But please note: this author chooses not to be dogmatic on this point, insisting this scenario will come to pass. Nor do I advocate that the Mark of the Beast necessarily requires some sort of genetic splice supplied by ET—perhaps constituting the DNA 'fix' that will wean us away from war, eradicate disease, cure a future plague, or even offer immortality. And I'm very reluctant to advise

Christians to avoid all vaccinations supposing that the 'mark' lurks within them. And yet, while I do not assert this scenario constitutes how the Antichrist will reveal his 'mark,' I confess, for the most part, I consider myself aligned with those who affirm that this ultimatum could await us. I judge it to be a legitimate possibility. So be advised.

On the other hand, I contend without equivocation that our centuries old captivation with the planet Mars and the Ancient Alien debate are prelude to the *coming great deception*, a deception hundreds of years in the making, a deception already partially in place but especially threatening as we rush into the 'singularity' engendered by massive, unrelenting change. The pace of knowledge acquisition is itself mind-boggling. Only the smartest among our race can begin to keep up with those changes, and then only if they specialize in well-bounded areas. Stephen Hawking says as much in his book, *An Illustrated Brief History of Time*. He goes on to state, "The rest of the population has little idea of the advances being made or the excitement they are generating." [5] Despite Hawking's confidence, caution best prevail over such optimism. Far more is at stake than just advancing technological knowledge of human physiology, and implementing the so-called mind-machine interface. We are edging closer to irreversible decisions on engineered heredity. Ultimately, at stake is nothing less than our identity as humans—indeed, it is our human genome that stands to be contaminated by 'fixes' whose implications remain impossible to foresee. The promise of today's *transhumanism* will not likely exceed its pitfalls. This is true whether engineered by human science or engrafted from extraterrestrial DNA. Dystopian rather than utopian outcomes could result demanding remedies beyond our ability to invent. Is it too crazy to believe such high strangeness could come to pass? Just remember, when Marconi submitted his discovery of the wireless radio to the postal office in Italy in 1895, the director scoffed "Straight to the Asylum!" When Marconi traveled to England in 1896, its postal officers were much more amenable to his invention and became investors.

There are any number of possible 'futures' that might transpire, likely predetermined by what we believe about our 'past.' Noted alternative historian (and conspiracy theorist) Jim Marrs in his recent book, *Our Occulted History*, argues an elite leadership exists in our world which knows the truth about Ancient Aliens. From his vantage point, the evidence compels him to assert these aliens have hostile intentions. Marrs says, "There is another narrative growing in public consciousness, that can no longer be written off as mere fable: the idea that aliens from outer space or another dimension may have— or may be trying to—take control of the world." Marrs claims that history, our history, is 'occulted' or hidden from us. The elite know the truth—but they keep it to themselves. "It would appear that something nonhuman seeks to control the planet Earth and may have even contributed to the advent of modern humankind." [6]

Given my findings (in the book *Lying Wonders of the Red Planet*) it seems noteworthy that Marrs begins his book's introduction with an extended quotation from American science fiction writer, H.P. Lovecraft's, *The Call of Cthulhu.* He also cites a lengthy passage from William Bramley's 1990 book, *The Gods of Eden* which more or less confirms the mostly fantastical convictions of Ancient Alien theorist Zecharia Sitchin:

> [Bramley] said he began studying the causes of war but came to the conclusion that "Human beings appear to be a slave race languishing on an isolated planet in a small galaxy." He added that "the human race was once a source of labor for an extraterrestrial civilization and still remains a possession today. To keep control over its possession and to maintain Earth as something of a prison, that other civilization (Bramley called them Custodians) has bred never-ending conflict between human beings, has promoted human spiritual decay, and has erected on Earth conditions of unremitting physical hardship. This situation has lasted for thousands of years and it continues today." [7]

This extravagant theory of humanity's condition, its origin, and the reason for our 'being born this way' (to employ Lady Gaga's lyric), hardly squares on all points with the biblical record. Nevertheless, it coincides in some regards: humanity remains a slave to the land-owner; Earth constitutes a prison for the commoner; most generally experience great hardship; we often serve the purposes of a kingdom of darkness; and our compromised condition has been ongoing without relief for thousands of years.

To advance this line of thought in biblical motif: there is an alternative proposal from a much more trustworthy source. His method to redeem our property and to save us from endless slavery mandates we forsake today's landowner and renounce his rule. For when we originally sold our deed to the property in exchange for a mind-bending upgrade (through our forebears Adam and Eve), the current landowner promised we would be 'as the gods, knowing good and evil.' Today, he still dangles a similar promise before us. If we will but follow his guidance, so he says, he will transform us into deities. In this respect, those who look to remedies from advances in genetic science (in the form of transhumanism) or ET (with his purported return), fail to detect the most sinister possibility that *the final planetary takeover may transpire when society goes 'all in' to force transformation—a mandated DNA makeover for all.*

Prometheus—Making a Man out of Clay

Classical mythology proposed that a Titan, *Prometheus*, teamed with Aphrodite to take a lump of clay out of the riverbed and fashion Adam. Adam literally means 'red clay' or 'of the earth.' The Greeks saw Prometheus as our creator and champion. According to their mythology, Prometheus gave 'fire' to humanity which represented intelligence, but more precisely, the development of civilization.

From the Greek, the name Prometheus comprises two words— *pro* and *manthano*—literally meaning "before intelligence." Prometheus also symbolized, however, a god of 'unintended consequences'—a tragic figure symbolizing humanity's questing for knowledge and striving to improve its circumstances. The image of

Prometheus has been employed in many different media to teach lessons about humanity, its origins, and its limits. Mary Shelly subtitled *Frankenstein*, "The Modern Prometheus"—and spun a tale forever forewarning us about the dangers of 'overreaching.' Goethe wrote his poem *Prometheus*, comparing his character Prometheus to the Son of God in the New Testament with Zeus as the New Testament Father, thus altering Prometheus from a Titan to an Olympian (by casting him as the son of Zeus).

Figure 14 - A Statue of the Classical God Prometheus

Fast-forward to modern day: in his 2012 movie prequel to the highly successful horror series of *Alien* films, Ridley Scott brought to the silver screen the mythos of an ET demi-god creating humanity through his movie *Prometheus*. What also stands out in Scott's film: the creator of humankind (*Alien* fans called him 'the space jockey') awakens at the prompting of a descendant of his creation, a mechanical masterpiece—the human-looking android (played by Michael Fassbender), also created in the image of his maker. The irony should not be lost on us. But the now alerted creator, the 'Prometheus' of the human race, becomes the crew's nightmare. (Of course, we had heretofore assumed the creator was compassionate). We learn that the financier of the outer space voyage has secreted himself away on the spaceship, seeking out 'Prometheus' on this distant planet that he might learn the secret of eternal life and be made immortal. Instead, the creator dispatches the decrepit old man (from a Judeo-Christian perspective) to *where he will meet his real maker*.

With 'Prometheus' awaking from aeons of sleep in 'suspended animation' on a planet far, far away, we are led to recall Lovecraft's Cthulhu, asleep in the darkest, deepest recesses of the ocean. Perhaps Kenneth Grant, the successor to Aleister Crowley and his black magick religion, Ordo Templi Orientis (OTO), was right in this one respect—all 'cults' are derived from one and the same story. Coincidentally, Ridley Scott's originator of humankind in the movie, 'Prometheus,' *happened to be a giant.*

Hollywood and the Remaking of Mankind

The barrage of alien movies continues unabated today. The movie *Cowboys and Aliens* (2011) by highly successful filmmaker Jon Favreau brought portions of Zecharia Sitchin's Sumerian 'Anunnaki' myth to audiences. The aliens were here to mine gold in order to save their world. Only the combined efforts of mega movie stars Daniel Craig and Harrison Ford could thwart their unwelcomed interplanetary gold heist.

The *Transformers* franchise has continued to thrill audiences with some of cinema's best-ever special effects. A recent chapter of the story, *Transformers*: *Dark of the Moon* (2011), links many of the ideas put forth by Mike Bara and Richard C. Hoagland to these 'now-you-see-them, now-you-don't' mechanical wonders. Even the so-called 'Secret Space Race' takes a bow with the less-successful-than-expected, *Apollo 18* (2011). Likewise, another franchise, *Star Trek* has been rebooted—again—with popular actors Chris Pine and Zachary Quinto in the roles of Kirk and Spock. The 2013 *Star Trek* film, *Into Darkness,* was a huge success demonstrating that audiences have not lost interest in achieving all-out victory in space. Humanity rules—Klingons best beware.

We could go on. Movie after movie propagate aliens, flying saucers, good extraterrestrials, bad extraterrestrials, and humankind's destiny in space. As a culture, we could hardly be more smitten with a scenario of the future. Indeed, the impact of film on the human psyche goes beyond these explicitly 'spaced-out' stories. The superhero genre almost always includes extraterrestrials in the plot. The elders among my readers certainly recall Superman battling his father's archenemies from Krypton, Zod and Company, in *Superman II* (1980).

Given that this constant bombardment surrounds us, do we suppose our children are immune to the dreams implanted in their minds by these most awesome tales? After all, what child doesn't want to run faster than a speeding bullet? Or be able to leap tall buildings in a single bound? Surely you get the idea. The *transformation of humanity into gods* is something that we live, sleep, and breathe in pop culture. Soon not one, but two generations will have grown up believing in *the viability of various ET scenarios and the desirability of becoming gods.* For decades, as far as alerting its members is concerned, the Church of Jesus Christ has been asleep at the wheel—or should I say, asleep at the spaceship console? The new promise of *becoming gods* has gone largely unanswered. The Church in Babylon languishes outgunned with such futuristic folklore.

Now, taking a step back: I judge the most likely reason for the reader to reject the thesis of this essay would be to assume that we simply have our minds on other more mundane, earthly matters. However, this conjectured counter-point falls short of a bona fide challenge given the prowess of the unrelenting, overwhelming message of movies, television, and a few Ancient Alien 'fact books' thrown in 'to set the record straight.' Furthermore, assuming that someday the mainstream media will pick up on the story (when the plutocrats give the 'OK' signal), we will be inundated with the idea our destiny does reside 'in the stars.' We will no longer be restrained and earthbound. We will soar to new heights—the sky will no longer be the limit. With that outcome, reshaping the collective mind will then be complete. No longer will ET need to set the mother ship on the White House lawn to impress. All we will require to set a celestial destination will be little more than a nudge. Should we stumble upon an artifact or two demonstrably evincing ET (the implications of the discovery will be drawn out to prove Ancient Alien theory), we surely will be more than captivated—we will be permanently marooned in the alien mythos.

But will that occur? Will alien archeology (aliens long gone) send civilization off in a new direction? Or will an intervening incident alter what appears to be the inevitable galactic fate of humanity? In any event, it appears that the old worldview of the common man and woman stands ready to be forever altered by a supramundane occurrence. It won't likely happen today—but it is coming sooner than you think. UFOs and alien abduction will be taken up by the mainstream media as news. Society will no longer associate these items with space cadets who wear tin foil hats. It will be adopted just as evolution was a century ago. When our kids ask us where we came from, it will be part of the explanation we teach our kids. If the Lord tarries.

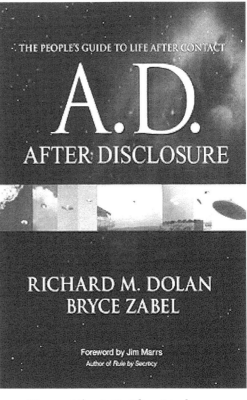

Figure 15 – A. D. After Disclosure

Does this seem too far-fetched? Consider the following update.

Disclosure—Will It Ever Happen?

So we come to the matter of UFO disclosure. UFO researchers (and Ancient Alien theorists) ask earnestly: "Will the governments of the world, most notably, the United States of America, ever admit that ET exists—that we have incontrovertible proof, and that (possibly) we already have a pact with alien beings?"

Richard M. Dolan and Bryce Zabel, in their 2012 book, *AD: After Disclosure,* describe the world AFTER the government tells us the truth about extraterrestrials. As is customary, the publisher pro-

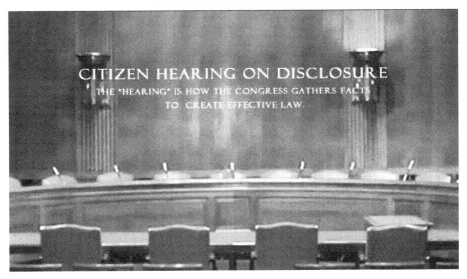

Figure 16 - The Citizen Hearing on Disclosure, 2013

vided numerous approbations to market the book. The contributors comprise a *Who's Who* in the UFO world. Jim Marrs (who also wrote the foreword), Nick Pope (the former Director of the U.K.'s research into UFOs), Stanton Friedman (perhaps the most scientifically competent and well-spoken advocate for telling the truth about ET), and Stephen Bassett (the most highly respected activist for disclosure), all shower praise on Dolan and Zabel's book, *A.D.*

Friedman comments, "Considering the overwhelming evidence that Earth is being visited by alien spacecraft and that many intelligence agencies and military groups have known this to be true for some time, we certainly need to consider the serious question of what happens when Disclosure actually occurs." Likewise, Stephen Bassett shares a similar conviction: "Disclosure, the formal acknowledgment by the world's governments of an extraterrestrial presence engaging the human race, *is inevitable*. So was this how-to book on what to do when a new world begins." [Emphasis added]

Just recently, Bassett achieved a true high-water mark for the whole topic of UFOs and government secrecy when he gathered all the experts together for five days of public testimony in early spring, 2013. *The Citizen's Hearing on Disclosure* obtained a level of credibility for the topic that surpassed anything before its conduct. From the official website, we read this summary of the event:

> From April 29 to May 3, 2013 researchers, activists, and military/agency/political witnesses representing ten countries gave testimony in Washington, DC to six former members of the United States Congress about events and evidence indicating an extraterrestrial presence engaging the human race.
>
> The Citizen Hearing on Disclosure was an unprecedented event in terms of size, scope and the involvement of former members of the U.S. Congress. With over 30 hours of testimony from 40 witnesses over five days. The event was the most concentrated body of evidence regarding the extraterrestrial subject ever presented to the press and the general public at one time. [8]

And yet, despite the noteworthy progress made by Bassett and Company, this author remains skeptical that the subject of DISCLOSURE will be broached by an official U.S. government statement anytime soon. As we documented concerning NASA (extensively discussed in *Lying Wonders of the Red Planet*), when our leaders evaluate the pros and the cons of earthshaking announcements they move at a snail's pace. Admitting intelligent life exists beyond our world becomes something of a "business decision." Is there more to be gained or to be lost by announcing ET to the Planet? Will higher-up government officials follow the lead of NASA Scientists and avoid declaring for or against the reality of UFOs? We have assumed these scientists suspend judgment publicly for self-serving reasons. Maybe it has been a ploy to keep the dollars flowing from Congress. Maybe the majority remain silent for career reasons. Then again, perhaps their rationale rests only in holding the majority view to present a conservative demeanor. Who can say? But political leaders will be no less "political" in determining what to say and when to say it. Of that fact, we can be highly confident.

Several governments in our hemisphere (e.g., Mexico and Brazil to name two), seem eager to disclose what they know. In contrast, just a few years ago our British friends took a passive approach when they released their UFO files to the public without any definitive conclusion. Their action amounted to a calculated decision that whatever the UFO phenomenon was, it no longer merited national funding and dedicated resources. ET was no longer a threat. Still, the U.S. government holds its peace. Will this ever change?

Perhaps a key principle of our government, the separation of Church and State, weighs on the minds of certain leaders. Maybe confirming the existence of aliens so threatens religious views and our societal self-image, our leaders suppose it is "not for them to say" whether ET should be "outed." Regardless of the conviction belonging to most UFOlogists (that is, that our government knows far more than it chooses to tell us), our leadership's reluctance to inform the public may only be fueled by a failure to know enough details concerning ET's status. Would our leaders want to broadcast what it knows about ET when it still does not know enough to assure the population that aliens constitute nothing of a threat? It much prefers to stroll along quietly "whistling in the dark." After all, normal human behavior for leaders includes avoiding any subject about which you know too little. In the government's defense, if it cannot claim to have "all the answers," better not to raise the subject at all. Otherwise it would invite public ridicule for failing to have mastered the details. It might only encourage anger and even panic if *Disclosure* occurs and the citizenry determines its leaders performed incompetently in the face of this potential danger. We know it is one thing to be caught off-guard. It is quite another to perform inadequate 'due diligence.'

On the other hand, if Jim Marrs is right and the elite of the world wish to continue holding all the cards—disclosing the truth about aliens (rather *what is believed to be true about ET*)—represents information threatening the status quo. What will the long-term effects be of such disclosure? Dolan and Zabel seek to answer this question, but the reality remains that the effects could be anybody's guess. Francis Bacon said, "Knowledge is power." Therefore, telling the truth might be seen as weakness—it could even be judged that the elite were forced to spill the beans. Egos at the top would never acquiesce to such plebian pressure.

Conclusion: Disclosure Bit-by-bit

In the final analysis, disclosure seems to be happening, slowly, methodically, without fanfare. Step-by-step, an awareness of alien existence, perhaps by the release of information about artifacts on Mars (as my book *Lying Wonders of the Red Planet* attests), will suggest that intelligent life (albeit not really extraterrestrial but *ultradimensional*) does exist elsewhere because we have proven it existed in the past on another world. Artifacts uncovered 200 million miles from home, dated from a million years ago are a lot less threatening than ET standing at your front door.

Stephen Bassett, in an interview conducted by L.A. Marzulli included in Marzulli's video (DVD) *Watchers 7*, supposes that disclosure stands to happen very soon. Once it does, Bassett concludes all that we will hear 24/7, will be ET. Our media will be consumed with the subject. It will change everything.

To my way of thinking, however, that sort of 'shock and awe' encompasses the strongest reason why it will *not* happen with a mighty splash. Disclosure will not be all at once. Too much change implies a disruption of public politics, social institutions of all kinds, and most especially, *the economy.* The elite may be many things, but they are not stupid. They have vested interests to protect. Making money remains their number one priority. They are not eager to lose one red cent.

Differing with the views espoused by many conspiracy theorists and certain eschatological experts, I do not believe that the hidden leadership of the world seeks chaos so that martial law can be invoked. This implies that, at present, the elite lack sufficient control over the affairs of society. But is that really what they believe? Granted, avarice assumes 'one can never have enough.' But how much control constitutes enough control? No doubt our civil leadership sees to it that the government stands ready to deal with all sorts of catastrophes that could undoubtedly disrupt the normal ebb and flow of life. That does not mean, however, they are actively engineering chaos.

The transition they seek, if I may speculate unreservedly for a moment, seems much more likely to be a peaceful transition. Why seek to gain greater control by compromising the control you already have? Inviting chaos is a risky game in which no one, not even the most capable of leaders, can guarantee the outcome. It is one thing to force chaos in order to justify instituting Martial Law. It is another thing to be taking massive measures to prepare for its necessity IF chaos ultimately comes. (The latter is what I believe has been underway for some time now by the Department of Homeland Security).

There is little doubt that the U.S. government has been whittling away at our national sovereignty in order to advance global governance. The U.S. led the League of Nations initiative. The U.S. funded the creation of the United Nations. The U.S. is the catalyst to bring about a functional (but not necessarily 'official') one-world system. As this author has argued (with co-authors Douglas W. Krieger and Dene McGriff) in *The Final Babylon*, the United States has indeed become the Babylon of the last days. Our policies are the de facto agenda for most of the world. Even China no longer lurks on the sidelines. By encouraging China's investment in the U.S.A., we have effectively made China complicit in our global program. By encouraging its financial bets be placed here, China has been co-opted. Why would China want the U.S. to default on its China-financed loans? It stands to lose too much. The remaining outliers like Cuba and North Korea are little more than a nuisance. Defeating ideology is not worth crashing the world economy. The only remaining obstacle is the Middle East. Once defused, no more big political bombs exist. Indeed, global leadership intends that wars occur only as a matter of choice and not of necessity, primarily to assure that the world economy stays in good working order and the rich continue to accumulate wealth. Any debate about whether this transfer of power endures today remains an unresolved discussion only for the uninformed, those so mired in daily affairs they are unable to raise their heads to look about, or those intentionally oblivious to reality. Those are the hard cold facts about the world we live in.

The subject of origins, the acknowledgement of the truth, the possibility that the masters of the human species may return to Earth (or the disclosure that they have been among us already), is clearly not the priority of human governments, especially the most powerful government in the world. Wanting to know where we came from remains a preoccupation of those *not* in power. It constitutes no more than a 'people's imperative.' We should not expect any favors from those who, at the highest level, reign over us. Whether we are talking about the U.S. government or the so-called shadow government that exists behind it, such information is available only on a 'need to know' basis—and in their judgment, we do not need to know.

In conclusion, the truth we require remains a truth that does not come from any human government. Our real hope lies elsewhere. As Christianity has maintained for 2,000 years, we are not citizens of this world but of another altogether. We are only passing through. The faithful are like Abraham the father of all monotheistic faiths. *"For he looked for a city which hath foundations, whose builder and maker is God."* (Hebrews 11:10) To look for an origin or destination *on any world other than the place which Christ has prepared for us stands as the greatest deception to which we can fall prey.*

Jesus comforts His disciples with these eternal words: *"Let not your heart be troubled: ye believe in God, believe also in me. In my Father's house are many mansions: if it were not so, I would have told you. I go to prepare a place for you. And if I go and prepare a place for you, I will come again, and receive you unto myself; that where I am, there ye may be also."* (John 14:1-3)

Even so, come Lord Jesus!

Notes

---

[1] Known as the *Marcionite* heresy, named after *Marcion*, its teaching proposed there were two gods... an evil God of the Old Testament—a most irascible, grumpy old chap—and the good God of the New Testament, portrayed by Jesus. Professor at both Oxford and Cambridge, Henry Chadwick called Marcion "the most radical and to the church the most formidable of heretics." See http://alexklimchuk.wordpress.com/2010/09/16/famous-heretics/. Manicheanism is similar in impact and thus often confused. It proposes that God has two sides... two faces. He is both evil and good. Both answers are unbiblical. *Yahweh, The Two-Faced God*, a book co-written by Joseph P. Farrell and Scott D. deHart (2012), updates this point of view blaming violence in religion upon all monotheistic faiths.

[2] Ontology is the study of existence or the nature of being. An ontological necessity would mean that a "thing must exist by the nature of its definition."

[3] This is the message of Tom Horn and Cris Putnam's book, *Exo Vaticana*. A highly recommended read. The Pope stands ready to baptize the Space Brothers when they arrive.

[4] These authors include Tom Horn, Steve Quayle, L.A. Marzulli, Douglas Hamp, and myself with the caveats I mention here.

[5] Cited by Marrs. Jim Marrs, *Our Occulted History: Do the Global Elite Conceal Ancient Aliens?* New York: HarperCollins. Kindle Edition, (2012), location 3626.

[6] Marrs, Jim (2013-02-12). *Our Occulted History: Do the Global Elite Conceal Ancient Aliens?* New York: HarperCollins. Kindle Edition. Location 122.

[7] Ibid. Kindle Location 171.

[8] See http://www.citizenhearing.org/.

The Ultimate Solution to Society's Unsolvable Problems

By S. Douglas Woodward

Be watchful, and strengthen the things which remain, that are ready to die: for I have not found thy works perfect before God.
(Revelation 3:2)

But the God of all grace, who hath called us unto his eternal glory by Christ Jesus, after that ye have suffered a while, make you perfect, stablish, strengthen, settle you.
(1 Peter 5:10, NASB)

This essay is drawn from *Blood Moon: Biblical Signs of the Coming Apocalypse*

IN THIS ESSAY, I DISCUSS THE MOST RECENT (AS OF THE TIME OF THIS WRITING) POLITICAL TRENDS PORTENDING APOCALYPTIC IMPORT. HIGHEST ON THE LIST, THE MOVEMENT FROM EXISTENTIAL DESPAIR TO EXPECTATIONS OF DIVINITY. HIGHLIGHTED ARE POPULAR ATTEMPTS TO REWRITE AMERICAN HISTORY. I CONCLUDE WITH A CALL TO ACTION FOR THE CHURCH IN BABYLON.

Global Crises, Catastrophes, and Cataclysms

WE LIVE IN TUMULTUOUS TIMES. WITH ONE CRISIS BUILDING UPON THE NEXT, THERE IS NO RESPITE FOR THE ANXIOUS. UNSOLVABLE PROBLEMS MOUNT. MATTERS ARE MADE worse as time goes forward. We cannot seem to quiet this tumult. Cable news incessantly broadcasts the latest developments, 24/7.

It remains difficult to get past the worst calamities. Not that long ago, Japan experienced a nuclear meltdown brought on by a

9.0 earthquake while it sought to overcome the effects of a killer Tsunami most of the world watched live on television. At least 20,000 Japanese were lost—entire towns were obliterated. Millions of Japanese will be affected by radiation in one way or another from the failed Fukushima Nuclear Plant. Today in the United States, we worry about the resulting effects of its radiation on our West Coast. Will the radiation contaminate crops in California and infiltrate the American food supply?

On the other side of the world, Islamic social unrest and wars in the Middle East continue to plague millions there. Muammar Gadhafi was killed by a revolt. Egypt has waded through two revolutions. And Syria continues to be a tragedy made worse with the passing of every hour. Over 100,000 civilians have been murdered by the government there. There is no end in sight to that civil war. Now the Middle East confronts what appears to be the most evil terrorist group yet: ISIS (Islamic State), a Wahhabist sect of Sunnis, decapitating or crucifying anyone who opposes them as they race across Syria and Iraq, driving toward their goal to establish a Caliphate across the Levant.

Then there is the ongoing Israeli-Palestinian conflict. It continues to fester even as these other stories occupy the headlines. Despite a peace accord announced by the current Secretary of State, John Kerry, Iran likely still seeks a nuclear weapon that threatens to throw the whole region into war. Israel seems destined to take out Iran's nuclear capability. After all, they have carried out the same tactic before in both Syria and Iraq. They are not strangers to preemptive strikes.

Virtually repeating the issues leading up to World War II, Russia has recently taken control of Crimea, and the Ukraine appears up for grabs. It is not clear why the U.S. government seems resolute in its poking Vladimir Putin, the Russian President, in the eye as he seeks to stabilize an ineffective government in a neighboring country full of Russian citizens. [1] But tensions rise nonetheless.

Experts comment that the United States has been seeking to build a democratic government in the Ukraine that could create a stronger buffer between Russia and the rest of Europe. Meanwhile, Putin seems to be attempting the same thing—building a buffer—because Russia has forever been fearful of what the Germans might be up to next. Memories of two world wars that killed tens of millions of Russians—wars started by Europe (and not Russia). Therefore, those wars and their lasting effects remain hard to overlook.

What's the World Coming To?

Lest we think we have only distant political problems with no effect on our daily lives in America or that our global challenges constitute only a temporary nuisance, intellectual 'think tanks' remind us that food shortages are with us to stay. The current rising cost of energy slows the chance for full economic recovery. Advances in medicine, information technology, communication, and agriculture all could back-fire as we introduce dramatic new technologies yielding unintended consequences. Future climate scenarios forecast stronger hurricanes, more extremes in temperature, and coastal flooding as ice packs in the Arctic and Antarctic relentlessly melt away. These grim prospects impact everyone.

In the U.S., the opportunity for improving our lot diminishes despite promises of recovery. Most Americans opine that the so-called *American Dream* died during the past decade. We anticipate our children will enjoy much less prosperity than what we have experienced—a gloomy expectation indeed never present before in U.S. domestic economic (and emotional) forecasts.

Over the past two decades, our popular culture grows increasingly edgy. Movies, television shows, and documentaries play on our fears, presenting catastrophes as entertainment. Disaster movies, frequently starring frightful aliens from outer space, are standard fare. Since entertainment comprises an escape from everyday difficulties, our captivation remains all the more surprising given these 'getaways' reinforce our helplessness against overwhelming forces apparently beyond our control.

We seek other kinds of relief in the strangest places with the worst substances we can manufacture. Our society has never been more addicted to hard alcohol, recreational drugs, overeating, consumerism, and sex. If we are not eating ourselves to death, we forfeit our future by purchasing ourselves into such deep debt that our only relief comes through extraordinary measures like default or bankruptcy. What is worse, our favorite pastime comprises staring enthralled at Hollywood celebrities doubling as icons for our moral breakdown. Their addictions and bad behavior feed our insatiable appetite for scandal. When one starlet dies from a drug overdose, another emerges to take their place on the road to ruin. Celebrities, to employ Elton John's magnificent metaphor, burn out like candles in the wind.

What can satisfy the hunger of our souls? Popular religions spin cosmologies more outlandish and over the top than ever. Pseudo-spiritual movements hype their mystical solutions for these tempestuous times. The 2012 phenomenon, now behind us, generated scads of books and self-help DVDs during the first part of the twenty-first century. Study shows, however, the core issue for those captivated by 2012 was not the end of the world, but the crisis of personal and political choice. In many ways, this 'movement' amounted to nothing more than a relabeling of new age pseudo-religion which dominated spiritual discussions during the last third of the twentieth century. Those that *tuned into* this new spirituality *turned on* to drugs, yoga, meditation, and spiritual disciplines whose practice promised *psychic reality*—a titillating 'high' absent in religious experience of common folk. Even more telling, belief in the supernatural grows exponentially. Movies and television shows based on the paranormal are now legion. The History Channel, that bastion of well-documented truths, celebrates belief in extraterrestrials as nurturing parents to the human race. UFO documentaries are replete with undeniable encounters of the unknown. How the scene has changed from the secularism and skepticism of the 1960s and '70s! Once upon a time, we strained to believe anything out of the ordinary. Now we accept whatever seems weird, whacky, and 'out of this world'—all in due course.

From Deadly Despair to the Delusion of Divinity

Underlying these gimmicks to discover life's meaning lurks a 'creeping death'—a deep despair regarding Western civilization rooted in our dissatisfaction with the old ways of thinking.

Decades ago (more than a century in Europe), we advocated principles originating in the Bible. We accepted a transcendent basis for law that guaranteed absolute truth. Practicing ethics in business mattered to most because we did not separate spirituality from secular pursuits. Since we accepted the notion of an all-seeing, all-knowing God whose laws demanded justice and compassion, we expended considerable time and effort in charitable activities.

Not that long ago in America, accountability was not consciously evaded but implicitly embraced. Taking responsibility personally or corporately to 'make things right' or 'do the right thing' was standard operating procedure for all but the most brazen business interests. Today, however, we first calculate the downside: "Why worry about it? To whom do we answer? If we can cheat and get away with it, why wouldn't we?" Ethics surely comprises an outdated concept if not a lost art altogether.

Nowadays, we much prefer to think of God as a reality 'residing within.' Harkening to ages old metaphysics, plagiarized from eastern mysticism then mixed with modern physics, we have chopped

God down to size. Our notion of God serves only as a subtle encouragement to be 'centered' and thoughtful—but primarily directed at the persons we care about most—*ourselves*. We have adopted a near-perfect pantheistic piety. Today, *it is all about us.* Consequently, when we choose to acknowledge the divine, we can now place His (his) name in lower case. What is more, since we perceive our deepest problems result from our failure to be *in touch with ourselves*, only *we* need take responsibility for our reclamation. By accepting our personal divinity, conventional wisdom now teaches we gain power to live, love, and be happy. Oprah makes us feel affirmed daily—everything is coming up roses! Better yet, that fascinating philosopher of Jamaican sound, Bobby McFerrin said it best in his 1988 hit, "Don't worry—be happy."

However, there are some gurus and spiritual guides who advocate a much more radical departure from our Western religious past. They promise new answers to satisfy our personal needs and rectify our political problems once we cast away the archaic notions of the *old order*—guidelines that are inflexible, materialistic, and legalistic. In some cases (such as in the movement self-named 'Awakening as One'), subtle threats laid buried within its hopeful but mystical message that challenged all inquirers to change to this new way of thinking or face the devastating consequences! Those who did not fall in line—who do *not* choose 'to sing out of the same hymnbook' with these pantheistic spiritualists—would not make the transition to the 'new age' (an epoch they incorrectly predicted to arrive on or soon after the end of 2012). The 'non-illuminated' were to be eliminated.

What were the means to exterminate the uncommitted? The answer remains unknown—the would-be 'next inquisition' toolkit was never disclosed. But since the philosophy behind this program was rooted in the same mysticism as Nazism (to be specific, esoteric *Theosophy*), a second holocaust might *not* have been out of the question for these activists. [2] It still lurks under other names. The messages broadcast from their website talked of an event reminiscent of a rapture in which those not inclined to advance into the new age will simply disappear from the earth. Poof! Universal forces magically eliminate the stick-in-muds refusing to transition.

Sizing Up the Real America

When we turn to social and political matters, do we find hope there? Are the old ways, those principles upon which America was founded, truly outdated? Is the dismissal of God from our government (virtually a *fait accompli* at this moment), likely to benefit our populace from whom the consent to be governed is derived? As a nation, do we still desire, "In God We Trust" to be printed on our currency?

Assume for a moment that Jesus Christ was invited to speak to a joint session of the United States Congress. Would He praise our government for the way it manages things? Or would Jesus challenge our nation's leaders to see the signs indicating America's future slumps toward demise? Would He praise us for our democratic ideals or rebuke us for our failure to live up to the principles our political philosophy advocates? Would He champion the American cause or criticize us for turning America's 'Exceptionalism' into a disingenuous ideal justifying whatever self-serving course of action we forcibly implement to further wrap the world around our little finger? Would He predict good times ahead or warn that the consequences of our chosen path portend calamity?

During 2013, Oliver Stone (a director not frightened by the prospects for confronting conventional wisdom), offered a ten program series entitled, "The Untold History of America." Presenting a multitude of matters glossed over by the standard history books, Stone argues conclusively that America feigns allegiance to democracy for the nations. Instead, it exploits opportunities predominantly to advance the aims of the 'military industrial' complex—corporations that make their living by producing munitions, often relying on the

CIA to exacerbate if not commence conflicts in 'hot spots' all over the world which eventually lead us into war.

This author has presented a series of books documenting many of the same points along with numerous others Stone does not mention, which exceed the worst case scenarios of what one could imagine a runaway government could engineer—all accomplished on behalf of furthering the American empire. *Power Quest, Books One and Two*, as well as *The Final Babylon (co-written with authors Douglas W. Krieger and Dene McGriff)*, all testify to the real agenda of America which consists in dominating the world and maintaining markets for America goods and services. The almost unanimous acceptance of our hard-nosed declaration that America no longer operates from a Judeo-Christian intellectual (or moral) basis has truly surprised my co-authors and me. Evangelicals, typically very conservative politically as well as theologically, have slipped into a growing malaise of disbelief in the inherent goodness of America. Ten years ago this was not true. It is true today.

What type of issues testify to the failure of the United States to be true to its founding ideals? Take the mission statements of The World Bank and the International Monetary Fund (IMF) (sponsored predominantly by America's bankers). These visionary credos read as if they sincerely seek to help the Third World in the same guise as the Marshall Plan helped a devastated Europe after World War II. Nothing could be further from the truth.

While doubtless the World Bank and the IMF have alleviated pain and suffering in some regards, they have placed all their customers in such a massive mountain of debt that these nations are forever 'beholdin' to the United States—more specifically to the bankers of the United States and England. Unending interest payments fuel the profits of the Anglo-Americans bankers whose headquarters reside on Wall Street or in 'The City' of London. Readers should be mindful that third-world countries that default on their debt (or second-world nations like Greece or Cyrus), hardly upset the equilibrium of international affairs or even harm their standing for continuing on the dole. Defaults are virtually meaningless as debt is simply refinanced and the interest payments commence once again.

Why do defaults matter so little? One must remember that 'the principal' for such debts was invented to begin with by leveraging the Fractional Banking System at the base of these machinations. The banks never lose real money. That is because the 'principal' is literally invented out of thin air. It is the greatest scam in the history of humankind. What is so pathetic is that most of humanity remains ignorant that they are being raped and pillaged by the rich.

Do Myths and Moral Lapses Cause Our Problems?

And yet, the citizenry as well as its leadership merit blame. The populace spends too much time caught up in 'life as usual'—soaking up entertainment rather than taking stock of what stands wrong with society and *how we can correct it.* Social responsibility stands in need of rejuvenation for our notion of freedom today infers the disregard of duty. Perhaps we consciously choose to ignore what is happening out of apathy; or worse, we do nothing because we have been brainwashed to accept 'it is what it is' with no recourse.

Another popular series of movies achieved some level of consciousness raising. The first film was entitled, *Zeitgeist: The Movie.* [3] The producer of the film, Peter Joseph endeavored to teach several fundamental truths.

First, religion is merely a means to gain social control. It instigates war and conflict. He argues we must realize that all religion is based upon sun worship and that each religion has the same identical 'solar savior' at its core whether its protagonist be Horus, Mithras, or Jesus Christ. However, Christians should not be fooled. The 'facts' presented are easily refuted by any credentialed religious historian. Nevertheless, the film mounts a compelling (although incorrect) *apologia.* [4]

Joseph next contends that we must face the fact that social engineering drives our government. He presents another overwhelming barrage of 'facts' on the tragedy of 911, demonstrating to the horror of the viewer that the U.S. government played no small part in facilitating the destruction of the Twin Towers under the cover of a terrorist attack. The smoking gun, as many other researchers and investigators have proposed, is the collapse of World Trade Center, Tower 7. The tower crumbled at the end of that fateful day as if the subject of a controlled demolition. The reader may remember that WTC-7 was not hit by a jet. It received some damage on one side of the building with the fall of the two mega-towers, but it was *purportedly* destroyed by fire alone, an outcome which caused architects and engineers alike to cast grave suspicion toward the truth of what really caused the building to collapse upon itself at near 'free-fall' speed—an impossibility without pre-set explosives facilitating a 'controlled' demolition.

Finally, Peter Joseph argued that the culprit we should rise up against is the *shadow government* facilitated by the Federal Reserve monetary system. The system thrives by creating scarcity, controlling the money supply, and—through intentional inflation managed by the central banking system—devaluing currency over time. The goal: make debtors and slaves of us all. Earning wages amounts to nothing more than a pittance to pacify us—a small payment in exchange for the slavery to which we have allowed ourselves to become obligated.

Society, Joseph argues, should not be based on money and debt, but on the abundance of resources. His is a picture of a utopian possibility built upon hidden confidence in the goodness of humankind. Freed from the tyranny of money and government controlled by corporate interests, human beings can create a society in which all prosper having the basic necessities of life available for free. This prescription for hope hardly constitutes a feasible remedy. However, because it builds upon a most problematic humanism, the potential to make an impact upon our society comprises a 'million-to-1' shot.

Is There Change We Can Truly Believe In?

For those who might challenge whether our plight is as dismal of Joseph asserts, we must at least admit that as it now stands politically, we are a nation divided. We debate almost every substantive issue with the outcome predetermined based on 'party lines' (i.e., whoever holds the majority wins). This 'double-mindedness' in America stokes the fire of distrust and contempt, reinforcing political paralysis. The only fix for what remains wrong with our political and social structures rests in a 'vocal majority' to emerge demanding real transformation; for only broad agreement can foster dramatic movement in our values. But can harmony be found? Can we discover common ground upon which to reform our government?

Unless dramatic modification in the viewpoints of a super majority occurs within our nation, hopes for change will remain ephemeral. Any real transformation must address (1) the moral fabric comprising who we are individually, (2) what values we extol culturally, and (3) what ideals drive our goals politically. Without focusing on matters both personal and social, we will not garner sufficient leverage to change course for the better.

Again, this is certainly where Peter Joseph's proposal for a just society breaks down. Human beings act out of self-interest most of the time. *We are sinners.* Coveting what someone else has is as much a part of our nature as other carnal appetites that require frequent satiation. Even if everyone were to have the 'bare necessities' we would grow to demand a standard of living that satisfied all our cravings, much of which entails stealing what someone else has to make it our own. An old and paradoxically worded adage remains true: *Nothing is ever enough.*

Nevertheless, our national *raison d'être* seems set in concrete. International government continues toward full manifestation. America's persistent economic and military strength guarantee its eventual achievement despite the desire of the 'rank and file' that we retain national sovereignty, disavow the authority of the United Nations, put distance between our country and other 'noble pursuits' (i.e., global initiatives) of well financed NGOs [5] and their expert social engineers. The elite drive toward one-world rule while the population waves the flag and chants "U.S.A." The two perspectives could not be more incongruent or misaligned.

However, we should not assume that the elite are solely motivated by greed and corruption. In their mind, the globalist agenda demands commitment. They believe this program holds the only means to world peace. Without a coordinated plan to bring the governments of the world together, war will rage and multitudes will starve. The master plan foisted by 'the Captains and the Kings' [6] seeks to make conditions better for everyone on the planet. At least that is what they tell us. But can an elite supposedly motivated by altruism and 'reason instead of religion' resolve our problems? [7]

Certainly, the sheep dare not speak against these unelected shepherds, lest we be accused of paranoia or intransigence. Furthermore, since most folk do not suspect the wealthy of such malfeasance, they remain mostly silent. So it should be no surprise that our government, supposedly of the people, by the people, and for the people, unwittingly and progressively relinquishes sovereignty to the elite few—believing that bankers, international corporations, NGOs, and media moguls will build a better world for us all.

An honest study of political science in the United States over the past 100 years shows that our Constitution, the high water mark of human government, no longer remains the bulwark against tyranny that our elementary schooling so naively promised it to be. [8] Unfortunately, politics and 'change we can believe in' will not likely lead to real change in our social order. While the poor and dispossessed will settle for any government that feeds and medicates them, most folk with just a modest education and modicum of social responsibility, do not expect government to change things. Past (poor) performance *does* predict future returns. A crisis of faith in our leaders and our system of government appears inevitable.

It is not that the Constitution of the United States does not deserve our oath of loyalty. It assuredly does and true patriots know this. However, many now realize that our leaders pay little attention to the founding documents of our nation anymore. They have become experts at circumventing the compact of the People.

- The current President issues Executive Orders (http://www.whitehouse.gov/briefing-room/presidential-actions/ executive-orders) working around the Congress—now over one thousand in number—exceeding all 43 other U.S. President's Executive Orders combined. On many matters, for all intents and purposes, he has become Caesar.

- Congress cannot agree on a budget to run the country. The legislative branch remains caught in a quagmire brought about by career politicians who get paid lots for accomplishing little.

- The CIA routinely breaks the law internationally, and likely conducts illegal domestic operations, while failing to obtain actionable intelligence on far too many matters. It is lucky that the nation has not performed a risk-reward analysis on their results.

- The NSA, always a questionable entity within our democratic society, leverages the Patriot Act to a breaking point, making a mockery of the constitutional privacy rights of the citizens. With safe-keeping like this, who needs the apparatus of a police state?

- Bolstered by their lobbyists, the military-industrial complex works overtime to ensure that our military fights endless wars. With over 1,000 bases located globally, we constitute the police of the world and comprise the enforcers for the New World Order.

- The State Department allows its officers in the Foreign Service to become pawns in international politics, intrigue, and secret strategies to overthrow other governments. The 2012 Benghazi scandal (the death of Christopher Stevens) is the latest case in point.

- The (now former) Attorney General runs guns in plans of which, at best, he is ignorant. Then he ignores congressional requests for information, stonewalls investigations, and selectively enforces laws that suit his politics. This was the essence of the notorious program now known as 'Fast and Furious.'

- The Supreme Court, when it must stand up to the obvious tyranny of the Executive Branch, backs away from the conflict and punts, resting upon a makeshift rule not written in the constitution: *elections have consequences!* Methinks this was actually a rejoinder boasting how Supreme Court Justices are certainly not responsible to the electorate—they can do or not do as they pretty well please. At the very least, the conservative Chief Justice chided us with the sentiment: "You have made your bed—now lie in it!"

To expand further on this last point: even if there are reasons to doubt the legality of legislation on nationalizing healthcare as structured in ObamaCare (a 1,100 page law passed so then Speaker of the House Nancy Pelosi could find the time to finally read it)—even if there are reasons to challenge the law since a virtual majority of the 50 States found the law impossible to implement—the last bastion of sanity, our Supreme Court, thanks to the failure of the recently appointed Chief Justice, refused to save us from a government run amuck. Millions of persons that were to become insured, weren't. And millions of others that had healthcare insurance, lost it and became the newly uninsured. Applaud the moral victory for the socialist planners serving at the pleasure of the President. [9]

Consequently, is there really any hope left that our government can correct its ineffectiveness and dishonesty, and get back to the business of acting on behalf of its patrons? As is often the case, real change happens when it constitutes the only choice available. Unfortunately, even if faced with the mandate for change, the rich and powerful will still come out on top. The best interests of the People are forever unlikely to be well-served—without a dramatic change of hearts.

The Only Hope—The Kingdom Of God Must Come

The Kingdom of God stands as the only hope for our world. This does not mean that there is no hope for change until Christ returns. Substantial change can occur, but only with dramatic differences in what should rightly motivate most people, those in key positions that have the power to influence material change in society. Believing in a purely humanist ideal—whether it be described as 'the audacity of hope,' 'hope we can believe in,' or realizing the 'divinity of human beings' (e.g., the 'new age' gospel)—remains destined to fail. Secular Humanism, based upon an unrealistic view of goodness in people, has never worked before and it never will.

The only manifesto that can achieve genuine change in society must be based upon the view derived from the principles of a Judeo-Christian cosmology (and the Gospel). These principles must be internalized by those who acknowledge them and pledge to follow them with the ongoing help of the Spirit of God. That stands as the biblical prescription for authentic and dramatic transformation in our world. Short of that, nothing will bring about meaningful change other than the apocalypse itself.

Christ calls His disciples, however, to model the Kingdom *today*, even though the ultimate fulfillment of that Kingdom will never be achieved until Christ dwells on this earth. Only when His will is done on earth as it is in Heaven, can we expect a perfect (or even a substantially better) world. Only when those who choose to be His disciples truly become His disciples—by giving up their lives for the sake of others, by electing not to place their financial well-being ahead of everyone else's, by treating others as they would themselves want to be treated—can we achieve a world that we would truly desire to inhabit. It would not be perfect. But as Christian intellectual Francis Schaeffer maintained, the world would experience *substantial healing* through the power of Jesus Christ. It would be measurable. It would be meaningful. And it would promise (through its portrayal) what the final state of the Kingdom of God would resemble. [10]

Christ taught that the Kingdom of God would turn the world upside down. Those that who were poor now would become rich. Those that are meek (and weak) will be powerful when the Kingdom of God comes. This will finally be realized in the Kingdom because those *that hunger and thirst for righteousness will be satisfied*. Only when the craving to live an exemplary life rises above other cravings in the lives of those in power, will social institutions change, and the downtrodden and dispossessed achieve an acceptable quality of life. The inner transformation must come first. Then outward transformation can take place.

The Lesson of Zacchaeus

Allow me to share a story from the Gospel of Luke to better explain how Christ's disciples are to understand the meaning and implication of salvation in the fallen world in which we live. In this account in Luke, we have a short-story about a very short-man named Zacchaeus. He was a *publican* (not republican, although if he were alive today, he likely would be one!) We understand this position was a public official, most likely a tax-collector. He was hated and was considered in the conventional wisdom of his day 'a sinner.' But his story illustrates the hope that an authentic representation of the Gospel of Jesus Christ offers to any society.

The account occurs in Jericho, one of the oldest cities in the world, the city that Joshua and the armies of Israel marched around seven times, before 'the walls came tumbling down' at the sound of their trumpets. Perhaps this particular venue was not accidental to the meaning of the story. We have an older man, a sinner, hanging from a Sycamore tree (sometimes a symbol of Israel), in Israel's oldest city. Could it be the change that occurs in the heart of Zacchaeus suggests that no matter how 'set in his or her ways' a person is, that no matter how old the institution is, or corrupt the politics of a particular city or state, transformation can still be achieved when the people in charge change? This constitutes part of the meaning that should be derived from Luke's tale.

We read, from Luke, chapter 19:

¹And Jesus entered and passed through Jericho.

² And, behold, there was a man named Zacchaeus, which was the chief among the publicans, and he was rich.

³ And he sought to see Jesus who he was; and could not for the press, because he was little of stature.

⁴ And he ran before, and climbed up into a sycomore tree to see him: for he was to pass that way.

⁵ And when Jesus came to the place, he looked up, and saw him, and said unto him, "Zacchaeus, make haste, and come down; for today I must abide at thy house."

⁶ And he made haste, and came down, and received him joyfully.

⁷ And when they saw it, they all murmured, saying, "That he was gone to be guest with a man that is a sinner."

⁸ And Zacchaeus stood, and said unto the Lord: "Behold, Lord, the half of my goods I give to the poor; and if I have taken anything from any man by false accusation, I restore him fourfold."

⁹ And Jesus said unto him, "This day is salvation come to this house, forsomuch as he also is a son of Abraham."

¹⁰ For the Son of man is come to seek and to save that which was lost.

As a token which expresses that salvation has come to Zacchaeus, Jesus indicates he has become 'as a son of Abraham' (in good standing no less!) Of course, virtually every race living in Israel (not just the Hebrews who traced their lineage to Jacob) were racially children of Abraham (coming as they did from Ismael or from Isaac, then from Jacob or his brother Esau). The Jews considered themselves God's chosen because they were *children of Abraham* (Luke 3:8, John 8:39). Jesus celebrates Zacchaeus reclamation by reaffirming that he was 'included back in the fold' just like any other good child of Abraham. He proclaims that an inner change has truly occurred. Salvation has come to the place where Zacchaeus lives (not just a particular house mind you, but through his actions—how he *lives in his community* from now on). That is, repentancc has led to a reform, because Zacchaeus will hereafter alter how he accomplishes his duties of political office.

Occupy Until I Come

But the lesson is not yet complete. Jesus spins a parable on the spot to explain the timing of the Kingdom of God and the responsibility to accomplish the Kingdom's work even while the King remains far away in a distant country. It also involves public officials. The parable was no doubt told when Jesus ministered in Jericho, since contemporary issues gave rise to the details of the parable.

The background of the story: Jericho was the hometown of Herod the Great and his son Archelaus. Jericho was where Archelaus had rebuilt his palace not long before Jesus sojourned to Jericho. However, Archelaus was not there when Jesus was teaching. He had left to go to Rome to receive his kingdom *officially*. And just as the nobleman in the parable meted out funds to each of his servants, Archelaus actually left money in trust with his servants to keep the business of the estate going. To 'occupy until I come' was likely a contemporary catchphrase conveying that the servants should busy themselves by completing tasks pertinent to the affairs of the estate. In Archelaus' case this may have included activities in the community no doubt partly related to the 'state,' i.e., its governance.

¹¹ And as they heard these things, he added and spake a parable, because he was nigh to Jerusalem, and because they thought that the kingdom of God should immediately appear.

¹² He said therefore, "A certain nobleman went into a far country to receive for himself a kingdom, and to return.

¹³ And he called his ten servants, and delivered them ten pounds, and said unto them, 'Occupy till I come.'

¹⁴ But his citizens hated him, and sent a message after him, saying, 'We will not have this man to reign over us.' [Which happened as the citizens of Jericho sent a message to Caesar complaining of the horrible actions of Archelaus and their plan to reject his rule.]

¹⁵ And it came to pass, that when he was returned, having received the kingdom, then he commanded these servants to be called unto him, to whom he had given the money, that he might know how much every man had gained by trading.

¹⁶ Then came the first, saying, 'Lord, thy pound hath gained ten pounds'.

¹⁷ And he said unto him, 'Well, thou good servant: because thou hast been faithful in a very little, have thou authority over ten cities.'

¹⁸ And the second came, saying, 'Lord, thy pound hath gained five pounds.'

¹⁹ And he said likewise to him, 'Be thou also over five cities.'

²⁰ And another came, saying, 'Lord, behold, here is thy pound, which I have kept laid up in a napkin:

²¹ For I feared thee, because thou art an austere man: thou takest up that thou layedst not down, and reapest that thou didst not sow.'

²² And he saith unto him, 'Out of thine own mouth will I judge thee, thou wicked servant. Thou knewest that I was an austere man, taking up that I laid not down, and reaping that I did not sow:

²³ Wherefore then gavest not thou my money into the bank, that at my coming I might have required mine own with usury?'

²⁴ And he said unto them that stood by, 'Take from him the pound, and give it to him that hath ten pounds.'

²⁶ For I say unto you, That unto every one which hath shall be given; and from him that hath not, even that he hath shall be taken away from him."

Like the nobleman in the parable, Archelaus was hated and resented. His only right to rule owed to his inheritance. And in the end, despite this unfairness, the servants realized that they must give account to what they had done for the good of 'the household.'

The connections between Jesus' parable and the matter of how His disciples are to conduct themselves 'in the meantime' stands as our de facto manifesto. We must 'occupy until He comes.' We are to invest the gifts given us that there might be a measurable return on investment, one which allows praise be given us from the King at His greeting and invitation into the Kingdom. But above all, at this present moment, we are to share the 'good news' that Jesus comes again—and very soon.

How should you prepare? John tells us, *"But as many as received him, to them gave He power to become the sons of God, even to them that believe on his name."* (John 1:12) And later, *"He that believeth on him is not condemned: but he that believeth not is condemned already, because he hath not believed in the name of the only begotten Son of God."* (John 3:18)

Remember that the frequently heard verse most often cited in pleadings made by evangelists for those who do not believe—that they should repent and accept Jesus Christ—constitutes an invitation not to pagans but to the 'lukewarm' CHURCH at Laodicea. *"Behold, I stand at the door, and knock: if any man hear my voice, and open the door, I will come in to him, and will sup with him, and he with me."* (Revelation 3:20)

I implore you now, invite Jesus Christ into your heart. Believe... and become a true child of God today.

Notes

[1] My personal theory involves the U.S. as enforcer of the New World Order. Putin is not behaving according to plan and the U.S. is in charge of putting him back in his place. Down with nationalism. Up with one world government. Remember whenever the dollar is threatened, the U.S. military comes to the rescue.

[2] I discuss this in depth in my book, *Decoding Doomsday*, in the chapter on "Esotericism, UFOs, and Nazism." This suspicion was also advanced by the authors of *The Stargate Conspiracy,* Lynn Picknett and Clive Prince.

[3] There were a total of three movies: *Zeitgeist, the Movie* in 2008, *Zeitgeist, the Addendum,* in 2008, and *Zeitgeist: Moving Forward* in 2011. See http://www.zeitgeistmovie.com/.

[4] A formal, well-structured argument.

[5] NGO is a Non-Governmental Organization (NGO). Here is a definition from the NGO website: "Though it has no internationally recognized legal definition, an NGO generally refers to an organization that operates independently from any government – though it may receive funding from a government but operates without oversight or representation from that government. According to the University of London, the history of NGOs date back to 1839 and by 1914 there were already more than 1,000 NGOs with international scope. Today, there are more than 40,000 NGOs that operate internationally, while millions more are active at the national level. For instance, the Chicago Tribune reported in 2008 that Russia had 277,000 such groups, while India has 3.3 million. NGOs have grown at a phenomenal pace, especially in the last two decades, creating a need for millions of jobs – both paid and volunteer based. But the modern "non-governmental organization" as we know it today only came about with the establishment of the United Nations in 1945." See http://ngos.org/.

[6] A book by this title, authored by Taylor Caldwell, was made into mini-series in 1976. It was loosely based on the Kennedys and presented a case that financiers are the real protagonists on the world stage. Democracy is illusory.

[7] This comprises the stated goal of Freemasonry, Rosicrucianism, and other secret societies seeking world domination, however righteous they purpose their influence to be. The writings of Albert Pike and Manly Hall, 33° Freemasons, and intellectual founders of the 'Craft' as Freemasonry refers to it, make this goal plain.

[8] Unfortunately, our elementary school teaching on American history and civics, presented in rose-colored hues, stands as an scant education most have never surpassed.

[9] I happen to favor a national healthcare program. That is because I have no illusions about the philanthropic qualities of health insurance companies, the giant Pharmaceutical companies (so-called 'Big Pharma') and ambulance chasing attorneys. The existing system is corrupt, unnecessarily expensive, and unethically structured (with "tiered levels of care"—he who can pay most gets the best care). The U.S. Healthcare system is NOT the best in the world despite having some of the world's greatest physicians and nurses. However, the attempt of the current administration to change the system has made it, in my opinion, far worse. Little hope exists that the system will be changed in such a way to make it what it ought to be while protecting the fiscal interests of all involved. The fix is not pure socialism, nor is the approach solely free market (i.e., *laissez faire*). I am not smart enough to propose the structure. But I am smart enough to recognize the current system remains broken and Obamacare has made healthcare more expensive for most Americans and less effective for the majority.

[10] Of course, the reality of sickness and death would still be with us. The tragedies of natural disasters would still occur unpredictably, and harm would come to those who are its victims. But enormous improvements for the better could be accomplished this side of the coming of the Kingdom of God through transformed social institutions, sufficient charities to help those in need, and the means to pursue happiness as the "God-given right" Jefferson extolled in the Declaration of Independence.

Afterword

By Sharon K. Gilbert

Congratulations, you have completed a survey course of the most important issues facing Christians today. Many who call themselves Christians might never have bought this book, assuming themselves already possessing 'uncommon sense as relates to exopolitics, exoreligions, and even extraterrestrial revelations; masters of zeitgeist matters which 'felt' so familiar. Others might thumb through the index and congratulate themselves on doing so, assuming this cursory journey might suffice to prepare them for days ahead.

But not you. You clamor for more—for insider information and deeper, more thoughtful explanations of the chaos screaming all about your ears.

You, dear reader, have chosen well; and you have not only read, you've devoured, you've consumed and now sit satiated and wondering. And so you should.

But now what? Do you pat yourself on the back and proceed to live your lives as you have been? May it not be said that any of you should even ponder such foolishness for even a moment! By reading this book, you have received an education that primes you for a higher, more intense education; and it has prepared you for action.

S. Douglas Woodward and Douglas W. Krieger have stood as 'watchmen' in the finest sense of that difficult, often thankless calling, and as faithful lookouts they have in turn warned all of us regarding the state of our world and where we are headed. The vision that crests over the blood-red horizon before their astonished and weary eyes shouts of terrors yet unseen and promises woe for a world gone mad but hope for those who trust in the Savior.

Geopolitically, the year 2014 commenced the formation of a 'tetrad' of blood moons that bookend a season of chilling changes. Ill winds blow upon the four corners of the Earth, and hoof beats echo against an unyielding, iron sky. Biblical Prophecy has become the bane of many congregations, so it is unlikely that Christians will find such watchmen standing ready in their local pews. By reading this treatise, you have shouldered a responsibility to pass it on; to take it to heart; to rush forward to learn more, more, and yet more. Surely, this sampling from Woodward and Krieger has whet your appetite for, yes, more of their worthy writing, but more importantly MORE of CHRIST.

Prophecy is the meat of Holy Scripture. Most modern, seeker-friendly congregations crave sugary delicacies that tantalize the tongue, but quickly vanish from the mind, leaving us hungry for more and weakened in spirit. Turn away from such empty fare, dear reader! Fill your mind and uplift your spirit with the living Word, which can also taste sweet, but requires lengthy digestion, for prophetic language is dense, and rich, and provides the stamina required to stand against the buffeting winds of change that rake across our souls.

So, before you close this book, allow me to remind you of what James, the brother to our Lord, says to us in his epistle:

> *For if any be a hearer of the word, and not a doer, he is like unto a man beholding his natural face in a glass: For he beholdeth himself, and goeth his way, and straightway forgetteth what manner of man he was.*

> *But whoso looketh into the perfect law of liberty, and continueth therein, he being not a forgetful hearer, but a doer of the work, this man shall be blessed in his deed. (James 1:22-24)*

The world is a mess, and it is getting worse by the day. The men and women who craftily shape opinion while reshaping our reality do not want to you to read this book, for it is a mirror that reveals the world as it truly exists. *Uncommon Sense* is a true mirror; an honest collection of essays that reflect and reveal the treachery, greed, and snares meant to trap you and trick you into believing the enemy's lie. As Americans, we have been indoctrinated with teachings that forever couple Christianity to patriotism. One cannot be one, *without being the other*. And so, it is painful to view the contortions reflected within this glass of this book's pages.

It is like the short story by Oscar Wilde, "The Picture of Dorian Gray." In this foreboding tale, a handsome and wealthy socialite gentleman sits for a painting by Basil Hallward, a downtrodden but talented artist who is infatuated with the beautiful Mr. Gray. Enticed into a life of hedonism, Dorian Gray vows to pursue only 'beauty,' assuming himself to be the epitome of such and longing to remain so. To accomplish this supernatural feat, he sells his soul in exchange for eternal youth and charm. So it is that each time Gray sins, the magical portrait grows more and more grotesque; each day he ages, it is the painting not the man who shows it. Hungry to pursue his evil lifestyle to its ultimate ending, Gray commits every sin he can imagine, including murder; and by the end of the story, the infamous painting has grown disgustingly and wretchedly deformed.

Perhaps, that is how you and I have been programmed to 'see' our nation and even our world—as the epitome of equality and justice, and power. We are, after all, one nation 'under God' are we not? Our country is special, Christian, and filled with alabaster cities. We are the protectors of the weak; promoters of peace and democracy.

We are beautiful, ageless, and without sin.

But it is all a lie. By reading this book, you been given access to the painting that has been hidden away in our nation's attic. It is twisted with vile conspiracies, and it is stained with innocent blood. This image, this true vision of what the enemy has done with our country should prick at your soul, as it drives you to your knees. But do not leave this mirror and forget what you have seen. Prophetic words can challenge us, inspire us, perhaps even terrify us, but they ultimately must propel the faithful *to act*. Not one of us is promised another day, so let us not squander these precious moments given to us today; rather, let us serve Him, honor Him, and lift up Christ crucified, risen, and coming again with every fiber of our beings.

My sincerest thanks go to Doug Woodward and Doug Krieger, two wonderful brothers in Christ, who doggedly remain standing upon that battered, broken wall, their unblinking eyes fixed upon the horizon. Thank you Doug and Doug, for writing this book dear friends—and for many, many more. You have sounded the alarm. Now it is up to us to answer the call.

Sharon K. Gilbert

Co-Anchor, PID Radio

Author, *Ebola and the Fourth Horseman of the Apocalypse*

Charleston, Illinois.

September, 2014

Appendix
Filling the Void – Prophecy Buffs
Need Community Too

By S. Douglas Woodward

The Quiet Minority

Over the past five years, I have had the privilege of being a speaker at a number of conferences dedicated to Bible prophecy. Prophecy enthusiasts ('buffs' [1]) come to such conferences—and do so with frequency. I have had the chance to meet many people who stop by my table to buy a book or just chat. Consequently, I see many of the same faces from one conference to the next. During this time, I developed some terrific friendships with many of these frequent attendees. For me, 'reconnecting' remains one of the best aspects of doing these conferences. Despite the gap of six or twelve months between meetings, familiar faces light up when eyes meet. The friendship almost instantly rekindles. Reconnecting brings genuine spontaneous joy. It may or may not be the primary reason we anticipate going to prophecy conferences; however, upon reflection we realize it comprises a major part of the experience that draws us to such events. Yes, we are eager to hear great messages and make new discoveries. Some want to shake

---

[1] The term 'buff' is most often applied to movie fans who know a lot about their subject. The term originally referred to admirers of New York City firefighters who wore buff (calf leather) uniforms. But it can be a term for anyone who gains detailed knowledge of a popular topic.

hands with an admired author or scholar. And yet, meeting new friends and seeing old ones provides the most long-lasting and meaningful reason for being there.

As you can imagine, there are lots of comments made about various matters. One of the most frequent statements I hear has to do with a particular 'pain point' that many feel after being at a conference for day or so. Perhaps the most oft-repeated statement attendees utter at my book table goes something like this: "We just don't get this kind of fellowship at our church. Members of our church don't know about prophecy and don't seem to care about it either." Or someone else puts it this way: "Our preacher doesn't talk about eschatology. It is too controversial. Why don't others find it important and want to know more?" Then there are some that admit "We just don't go to church anymore. We can't find one that teaches us about these things. We feel isolated and alone in our city. We come to a prophecy conference like this one to get energized and remind ourselves that we are indeed part of the body of Jesus Christ."

Surely the lack of frequent fellowship with other like-minded believers lies behind this lament. Those who go to a prophecy conference are a quiet and tiny minority. In contrast, attendees at a sporting event number in the tens of thousands and are highly vocal. They even paint their faces, wear stupid clothes, and act like idiots. But the audience of any given prophecy conference is unlikely to reach 1,000. Enthusiasm is generally muted, but underneath the outward demeanor there lies great hope and sometimes exhilaration. That inner excitement stems from being with others that care about the very same things that matter to us.

A Supernatural Experience

I must admit that I when it comes to 'going to church,' I have been a slacker. Since moving back to Oklahoma over a year ago, I have not joined a 'local assembly.' There are some great churches here and I need to join one soon. But one thing that holds me back: the nagging fear that what I teach and believe isn't likely to be embraced by those who lead such an assembly. I worry that I won't be accepted because I am too emphatic about the coming apocalypse.

Indeed, there is something going on with me and many others who believe like I do. It has to do with what I wrote about in my last book *Blood Moon: Biblical Signs of the Coming Apocalypse*. What is that issue? It's this: believers in Bible prophecy feel strongly that eschatology constitutes a crucial aspect of the gospel. If fellow Christians in our church or neighborhood fail to recognize that these days are the last days before Jesus Christ comes, we grow frustrated and feel (to use that philosophical word made famous by Karl Marx) 'alienated.' We want to experience real kinship based upon deeply shared beliefs. Sociologists may dismiss this motivation and condemn us for seeking merely to overcome 'cognitive dissonance'—which is an academic way of asserting that we need one another to reinforce our faith when events unfold in an unfavorable way, *challenging what we believe.*

But there is more to it than that. It isn't just the drive to eradicate annoying doubts that creep in when life throws us a curve ball. We crave *experiencing real joy*—the kind that the Spirit of Christ brings to an assembly gathered in His name. The Greek word is *koinōnia*—which conveys *intimacy and communion.* Paul provides his benediction in 2 Corinthians 13:14 with these words: *"The grace of the Lord Jesus Christ, and the love of God, and the* **communion** *(koinōnia) of the Holy Ghost, be with you all. Amen."* John the Apostle says this, *"But if we walk in the light, as he is in the light, we have* **fellowship** *(koinōnia) one with another, and the blood of Jesus Christ his Son cleanseth us from all sin."* (1 John 1:7)

All of us seek to be with people that share common experiences and beliefs. We are uncomfortable to be without the company of other believers that think like we do. Another more positive way to say it: we seek the comfort that comes from engaging with friends that affirm a shared faith and outlook. We refresh our hope and reinforce our confidence when we gather together. We have a deeply ingrained need to be among those that profess our perspective about the meaning of life. We need to gain consensus on how to interpret the crazy events of this world. We want to affirm that God remains vigilant over each of our lives and remains at work achieving His purposes amidst the otherwise unfathomable circumstances in which we frequently find ourselves.

However, it is *the supernatural connection we share which undergirds our communion.* The Spirit of Christ dwells in us and rejoices when we are together. For while we commune with one another we also commune with the Son of God and the Father. John relates this through this statement: *"That which we have seen and heard declare we unto you, that ye also may have fellowship* (koinōnia) *with us: and truly our fellowship* (koinōnia) *is with the Father, and with his Son Jesus Christ."* (1 John 1:3) Community extends into the heavenlies.

Thinking Counter to the World around Us

Eschatology advocates require this fellowship more than most. Why is this so? Because our beliefs run so counter to the mentality of this world. I wager very few readers enjoy the frequent company of those who regard what is happening in the world as evidence that the 'the last days' are upon us. The standard point of view, aka *conventional thinking*, remains as follows: "Times are tough, but we'll get through it... we always have before... today is no different." However, if you believe as do I that the state of our world surpasses anything that has come before now, that the current course of events will not work out so well for society or the human race in general (that this evil age is in fact coming to a conclusion), your friends probably regard you as a kook. Your family may ostracize you. You work buddies won't want to hear anything about why the apocalypse is at hand. Sure, they may just 'poke fun' at what you believe—but whether subtle or outspoken their disdain usually becomes apparent: they judge you the *odd man out*. And this sentiment can grow much worse. In fact, you might even come to feel personally threatened if you bring up the subject or offer your opinion with apparent conviction.

For example, I have an email 'pen pal' in Boston that was fired from a noted university for talking about his belief that Jesus was coming soon. He shared his faith with many co-workers. He led a Bible study. The administration told him to stop talking about Jesus and the end of the world. He refused. After this went on a few months, he was finally fired. Surprisingly, he sued the school and after months of deliberations he ultimately won his case. He was awarded with back pay and damages for having being dismissed without cause. I must admit, I was stunned. I thought he didn't have a prayer (although many were praying for him!) After all, he was 'fighting city hall' (or more specifically, a revered university). Happily this brother stuck by his guns and won his case. I'm happy to report he continues to this day sharing his beliefs and shining as a beacon for Christ. To be sure, his story stands out as *one of only a few* victories in the work place where Christian beliefs weren't trampled. Nonetheless, it encourages me.

Needing Ongoing Support

If you believe in Bible prophecy, you need ongoing support. For most, coming to a prophecy conference once or twice a year simply isn't enough. If you are one of the fortunate few that attend a great fellowship where the minister preaches eschatology, then your need for this sort of comradery is likely being met. Good for you—really. However, I suppose that less than one in ten persons who attend a prophecy conference enjoys such a pleasant and affirming situation. If you are one of the nine who don't, what should you do to galvanize your conviction and benefit from the joy of joining others who profess a similar apocalyptic belief system? Up to now, there hasn't been a particularly good solution. Consequently, I decided that something had to be done.

I joined with four other staunch believers in the soon return of Jesus Christ to launch a new ministry. Like me, they preach, teach, and exhort others on matters of Bible prophecy. Together, we have created a ministry we call simply, **The Prophecy Forum** (www.theprophecyforum.com). We announced this new entity on August 25, 2014. I encourage you to go to our site and read the announcement. Also watch a 45-minute video where we introduce our ideas about what this ministry should provide and why our team has the means to pull it off.

There are a number of reasons why we came together to form this ministry. One of the most important was recognizing that we should do more than just set up and speak at another prophecy conference and sell our books or DVDs. Instead, w*e must find ways to create community for like-minded brethren.* We must develop the resources providing continuity and consistency for those that participate in The Prophecy Forum.

One of those strategies involves utilizing social networking to enable such community. Since social networking reaches out globally and connects almost instantaneously to anyone 'attached' or 'online,' we will build what amounts to a global network of believers that anyone, anywhere in the world can join or participate at whatever level suits their need.

Certainly, we are hardly alone exploiting these technologies. There are many doing the same thing, some on a grander scale and perhaps for other good reasons. However, our rationale consists of the following: we hope to grow a community that regularly attends our forums in person or via live streaming (we plan on having about four to five events scattered across the USA every 12 months). Additionally, we will create a forum for conversations among those who are part of the community (using Facebook or

Google Circles) to keep our 'members' connected. Most importantly, we will supply resources to enable so-called *house churches* composed of as few as 4 believers and as many as 40 participants who gather in person anywhere in the world.

Exactly how each group structures their worship or engages in a Bible Study remains entirely up to them. Our offering will be to supply teaching and connection to form a 'movement' of sorts—one based upon a biblical mandate to preach the coming of the Kingdom of God, that proclaims Babylon is falling, that the Church of Jesus Christ must witness against the world system which opposes the God of the Bible, that individuals must repent and believe in the name of the Lord. Old fashioned ideas like sacrificial atonement, the deity of Jesus Christ, the infallibility of the Bible as our only guide for faith and practice, and finally the priesthood of all believers—these great doctrines of Christianity should be upheld and once again serve as the foundation for the Church *especially in these last days.*

For the past 15 years or longer, the most famous Megachurches have been taking their members in the wrong direction: seeking personal prosperity, acquiring happiness as top priority, achieving worldly success by flourishing within the 'system,' and aiming to impact society by being 'attractive agents' for Christ. This trend may not be reversed before the Lord returns—but it must be challenged.

Structuring for Activism

Chuck Missler, in his recent essay published in Tom Horn's *Blood on the Altar: The Coming War between Christian versus Christian,* speaks precisely to this point. Missler sees that traditional Churches are not structured to take on the status quo. They get 'wrapped around the axle' because financial stability is their top priority and they deem their not-for-profit (501c3) status mandatory if they are to stay viable and keep their doors open.

Pastors get caught up in church growth to expand their financial well-being, not necessarily to build stronger disciples.

Along with Missler, we look at the conventional church model and believe it now amounts *to a muzzle order.* To retain 501c3 status, Churches must avoid being 'political' and stay in their religious sphere of operation. They cannot side with one political party against another. They must be very cautious to not attack the President or his Cabinet members. They must watch their steps very carefully so they don't run afoul of the current administration. If they transgress, the IRS might just swoop in and cancel the offending entity's 501c3 status. So much for free speech. "You've said too much. We must keep you from disrupting peace and tranquility in our society." So the government pulls the trigger. Bang! You're dead!

Along with my friend Doug Krieger (a co-author of *The Final Babylon* and fellow leader in *The Prophecy Forum*) we also provided an essay for Tom's book. In our chapter, "When Antichrist Appears in America, Will We Recognize Him?" we discuss how the threat of losing not-for-profit status amounts to the same approach Adolf Hitler used in Germany to silence opposition from either the Evangelical (Lutheran) Church and the Roman Catholics. By splitting the spheres of religion and politics, Hitler co-opted the most likely source to challenge his racial agenda, oppose the Third Reich's destruction of liberty, and keep blatant Teutonic paganism from gaining control of the country. As the U.S. Federal Government grows increasingly hostile to Christians, we see the same cooption happening in America. Christians are often deprived of free speech and rights of assembly in public places like schools. Christian holidays are no longer respected. Incredibly, even in my 'Bible Belt' hometown, Oklahoma City, we are allowing a Black Mass at our Civic Center Music Hall in September, 2014, where I used to go to watch circuses and concerts. What has happened in our society that we would allow this satanic ritual in the

heart of our cities but stop the exercise of religious observances in government buildings?

The evidence mounts up: appointed political leaders in the Executive Branch and the Courts grow ever more emboldened in their efforts to protect secular humanism and heathen cults while Judeo-Christian principles are downplayed or overturned (despite the fact that such principles lay behind the creation of our revered form of government).

Getting back to Missler: Chuck recommends Christians form house churches, mirroring the informal structure of the early Church. In this format, leaders of the assembly have 'day jobs' while pastoring becomes their 'after hours' vocation. They don't draw the majority of their pay from the community they serve. By reducing the challenge to finance their church leadership, members eliminate the leverage that Federal or State governments have over their assembly. Collectively, the Church can then take stands against government policies or programs that it deems to be a challenge God's law or conflict with biblical principles. For too long the church has operated under the dictum, "If you can't beat'em, join'em!" We have adopted the ways of the world. There remains no visible distinction. Christianity and the Church no longer provide an alternative way of living that meets the demands of the Gospel of Jesus Christ.

Therefore, if we are to regain our 'saltiness' it requires we restructure. For many of us, we must forsake the conventional church model. We must adopt a new form of *polity* (how we organize ourselves). To be clear, how we structure the Church becomes critical to whether or not we impact a fallen world and fulfill our mission to make disciples in all nations. (Matthew 28:19,20)

Conclusion

To conclude, may we come to recognize that we are not alone, that we can band together across regions, states, or even nations to be members of a truly substantial group—one that has cohesion across all boundaries. No matter how widely separated we may be physically—spiritually, through Jesus Christ, we compose one body and one fellowship. On the local level, even in a small house less than one dozen strong, we must get comfortable with the fact we compose a legitimate part of the Body of Christ. Additionally, let us celebrate that such a 'low overhead' structure can equip us like never before to bring the gospel to our world, untethered to constraints that compromise our Lord's message and that liberate us to speak the truth with boldness. Lastly, let us never forget it is in community where we not only reinforce one another's faith. We encounter God the Father and the Son, through the fellowship of the Holy Spirit who dwells within each of us. Through the *koinōnia* of the Holy Spirit, Jesus Christ manifests Himself as we join together in His name. *"Where two or three are gathered together, I am in their midst."* (Matthew 18:19-20)

About the Authors

S. DOUGLAS WOODWARD is an author, speaker, and researcher on the topics of alternative history, the occult in America, and biblical eschatology, with 40 years' experience in researching, writing, and teaching on the subject. He is President of the Prophecy Forum. He co-authored *The Final Babylon* with Douglas W. Krieger and Dene McGriff. He has written eight books besides the present volume: *Are We Living in the Last Days?* (2009), *Decoding Doomsday* (2010), *Black Sun Blood Moon* (2011), *Power Quest, Book One: America's Obsession with the Paranormal* (2012), and *Power Quest, Book Two: The Ascendancy of Antichrist in America* (2012), *Lying Wonders of the Red Planet: Exposing the Lies of Ancient Aliens* (2014), and *Blood Moon: Biblical Signs of the Coming Apocalypse* (2014). Doug has also served as an executive for Microsoft, Oracle, Honeywell Bull, and as a Partner at Ernst & Young. He has served as Elder in the Reformed Church of America and the Presbyterian Church.

DOUGLAS W. KRIEGER is co-editor of the Tribulation Network (Tribnet) since 2004, having written scores of e-books on Bible Prophecy. He is a Director of The Prophecy Forum. He co-authored *The Final Babylon: America and the Coming Antichrist* with Dene McGriff and S. Douglas Woodward. He is author of *Signs in the Heavens and on the Earth* and *The Two Witnesses*. He has served as Education Administrator for public schools for 20 years, as well as Public Relations and (formerly) the Executive Director of the National Religious Broadcasters National Prayer Breakfast in Honor of Israel during the 1980s. He holds a BA/Admin. Cred, from CSULA/CSUS. Additionally, he was a pastor during the *Jesus Movement.* Since 1968, he has been married to Deborah and has three children who love the Lord Jesus. Doug's involvement in Christian Leadership led to several White House briefings during the Reagan Administration with the Religious Roundtable and the American Forum for Jewish-Christian Cooperation.

Made in the USA
San Bernardino, CA
27 May 2015